—HOW TO PAINT & DRAW—

PEOPLE

Written and Illustrated by Samuel Marshall

Victoria House Publishing

Acknowledgments

The Publishers would like to thank the
following for permission to reproduce
their photographs: The Tate Gallery,
London 6, 7 (above and below), 53,
64 (above), The Trustees of the National
Gallery, 52, 64 (below).
Illustrations pages 24, 25 T. W. Ward;
page 59, Nick Harris; page 58, Alex
Zwarenstein.
Graphic artwork: Terry Burton, Liz
Chapman, Imperial Artists.

Designed and produced by
Intercontinental Book
Productions Limited

Published by Victoria House Publishing,
Paulton, Bristol BS18 5 LQ

ISBN 0 907874 02 9

Printed in Hong Kong

Contents

Introduction

Whatever creative objectives are pursued by aspiring artists, and whether their approaches are conventional, stylized, distorted, or imaginative interpretations, an understanding of the basic principles of the human figure is vital. Whether they choose to adhere to, or depart from, the strictly representational, a thorough working knowledge of the human form will reinforce the value of their work.

This core of fundamental knowledge is something which has been developed through centuries of artistic endeavour, from the great Classical drawing masters of ancient Greece, through the creative giants of the Renaissance to the present day. These basic principles are not plucked from the air in moments of divine inspiration, but are the product of careful observation and meticulous visual analysis of the relationships between the many factors which work together to define form and volume.

The aim of this book is to define and explain these elements, to dispel the mysteries surrounding them, and to encourage the reader to develop both his or her skills and imagination. The greatest lessons, however, will be those learned through personal efforts and experience; the harder the reader works at his craft, the greater will be the rewards.

The purpose of drawing

The main aim of drawing is always to examine, in visual terms, the nature of the world around us. It is the outward manifestation of an analytical process through which we try to assess forms and their relationships one to another. The wish to draw begins with our interest in a particular object or form; we find it visually pleasing or fascinating or even puzzling. Perhaps we simply wish to record a particular moment of time, a particular movement, or even a mood. It can be an end in itself or merely the first stage in a larger study.

Whatever its final objective, drawing has to fulfill a number of very specific functions, and the drawing instrument is rather like a scalpel with which you dissect out those aspects of the subject in which you are specifically interested. As a place to begin understanding the purpose of drawing, look at as many examples of all kinds as you can find, and try to see in them what the artist was attempting to describe. Was he exploring the subject in terms of masses, that is, the large basic shapes which come together to form the subject? Was he exploring texture or the pattern of light and shade (tonal values) that are created by the subject according to lighting conditions?

Perhaps he was attempting to describe all or some of these qualities together. The more "finished" the drawing, the more things he is probably trying to represent. At this stage, it is useful to appreciate the difference between a sketch and a finished drawing. The former is

Right: *Sutherland's* Portrait of Somerset Maugham *is an almost linear drawing with the brush, echoing the very precise character of the sitter, enhanced by the elevation of his pose.*

seldom an end in itself, but rather a stepping stone to a more complete understanding of the chosen subject, such as would be found in a finished painting or drawing. It will, as a result, usually emphasize a particular aspect, such as mass or tonal range, to clarify the artist's understanding of that quality prior to his execution of a finished work.

Look also for technical drawings in books or magazines, for they are designed to do the same job although in a visually different way – that is, to explain the function of an object as a means of understanding it. Though extremely precise and clinical in style, it is as much a process of "dissection" as a preliminary study for a work of art. Once the selected aspect of the subject has been chosen, the draughtsman strips away, or ignores, everything else that is not relevant, in order to emphasize the essential nature of the subject in question.

Drawing is a way of bringing order to something. When setting out to draw a complex subject, like the human figure, it is difficult to know where to start, so try breaking it down into a few key approaches, such as the basic shapes of the various parts of the body, and sketch the flowing lines that both outline them and link them or half close your eyes until all you see are the areas of shadow contrasted with the areas of lighter tones and just scribble them in. In doing so, you are already beginning to use drawing correctly, as a tool for understanding.

7

Materials and media

The choice of media depends on what we wish to express in a drawing. The lead pencil is certainly one of the most versatile and convenient media, being obtainable in a wide range of hard and soft material, but it is important to experiment with other possibilities, as there will be instances where the pencil is inappropriate. Where a sharp, incisive line capable of subtle variations in breadth is required, pen and ink may be more suitable. Practise varying the degree of pressure applied and make use of the natural springiness of the nib to produce a line with "feel."

For a broader, sweeping treatment combining line and tone, try working with charcoal, conté crayon, or pastel, using your finger or an eraser to describe form by gradations of tone. Also try working on a variety of surfaces and papers.

Choose your materials

The drawing board
This should be robust enough to provide a stable platform for your drawing and the surface should be as smooth as possible, but able to take thumbtacks, clips, masking tape or scotch tape. Plywood or composition boards are usually cheaper than the special studio boards but do not easily accept thumbtacks. They are, however, generally lighter. The most useful size will take paper up to 24 by 36 inches.

Easels and "donkeys"
The simplest way of holding a board steady while standing is to have a loop of string which passes around the board and the neck. For working in one place the studio easel, which can accept up to 24 by 36 inches, is ideal while, for sketching, porta-

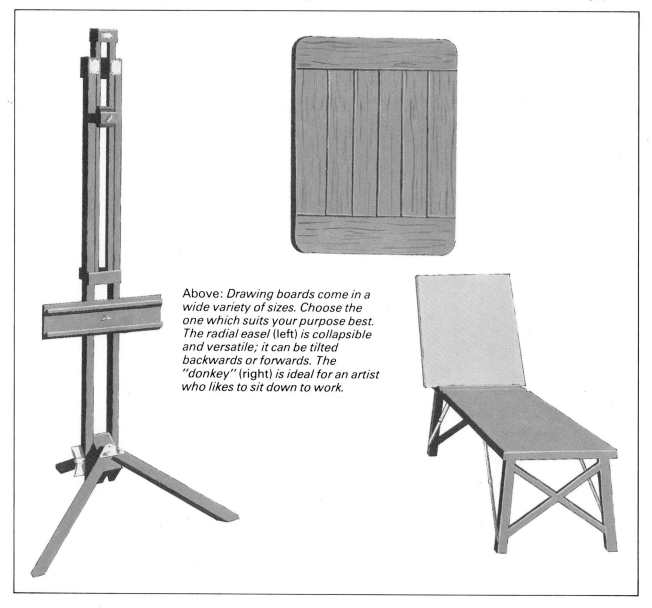

Above: *Drawing boards come in a wide variety of sizes. Choose the one which suits your purpose best. The radial easel* (left) *is collapsible and versatile; it can be tilted backwards or forwards. The "donkey"* (right) *is ideal for an artist who likes to sit down to work.*

ble easels are available which can take paper of the same size without difficulty.

Although the traditional studio "donkey" is a very convenient device which allows you to support your board and materials while seated for long periods, two chairs placed front to front are almost as effective.

Papers

Bristol paper is one of the most versatile and widely used papers for drawing and painting. Good-quality watercolour papers come in a variety of surfaces, often in pad form, and can be used with great effect. Make sure you use the right side, i.e., the side that the watermark "reads." Ingres paper is a subtly coloured paper with a fine texture or "tooth." Try this and darker-toned papers with charcoal or chalk.

Always buy a reasonable quantity so that you are not

subtle line-and-tone work rather than heavy, broad areas where charcoal or crayon might be better. Do not be afraid to use varying grades in a single drawing rather than forcing the blackness of the tones, which can produce a shiny effect.

The pencils shown here have been correctly sharpened with a knife rather than a pencil sharpener and have long, but well-supported points.

Chalks and crayons

Willow charcoal, sanguine, bistre and black conté crayons are also suitable for figure work. Conté crayons come in 3 grades and white. Like soft pencils they should be fixed to prevent accidental smudging. Pastel is a softer form of chalk used for painting as well as drawing. Coloured pencils are slightly greasy in texture and do not need fixing.

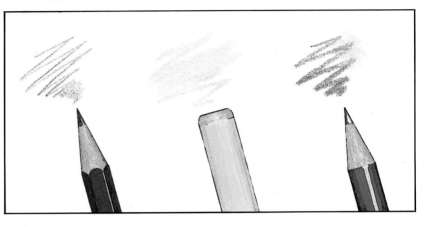

Above: *Coloured pencil, chalk and conté crayon. These can all be bought in a very wide range of colours.*

Left: *Examples of different grades of pencils. These samples show you how much variation there is in the mark produced.*

Below: *Samples to show the different colours and textures of paper available. The end result when using a medium such as watercolour will be affected by your choice of weight and texture of paper.*

2B   **HB**   **2H**

afraid to use it liberally. When using water with a medium, lighter-weight papers will need stretching.

Pencils

Lead pencils are the most common and can be easily sharpened. Their grades range from very soft and black to hard and gray. A good selection would include grades F, HB, 2B, 3B, and 6B. The precise nature of the marks they make encourages accuracy of observation and they are excellent for sketching. This quality makes them best for

Pens

These are drawing tools with a distinct individuality. The fact that they are indelible encourages a healthy discipline and confidence. They include:

Fountain pens These, particularly those able to hold black drawing ink, are extremely convenient, and the flexible nibs come in a variety of thicknesses and styles. They produce a strong, sensitive line that can be varied in thickness.

Stylus pens Favoured by technical draughtsmen for their clean, unvarying line, they come in a wide range of line widths and, like ball-point and fibre-tipped pens, have their own distinct and precise character.

Dip pens Still one of the most popular artist's tools, their flexibility and variety of line is unsurpassed.

Inks

There are many types and colours. When using ink with watercolour washes, make sure that it is a waterproof variety.

Oil paints

Oils are an ideal medium for finished figure paintings because of their malleable and expressive qualities. Unlike watercolour, oils can be more consciously manipulated and worked. Colours and tones can be worked into one another to produce a smooth and subtle transition which allows you to ''model'' the image on the canvas. It is also possible to build up the density of the pigment in a way which cannot be done with watercolour.

When faced with the enormous range of available colours and tints, it is difficult to resist the temptation to purchase a great number of tubes. Although it is certainly a matter of personal taste, the inexperienced student would be well advised to keep his palette to a minimum, and a useful selection would be as follows:

Flake White
Chrome Yellow
Yellow Ochre
Light Red
Vermilion
Alizarin Crimson
Terra Vert
Cobalt Blue
Ivory Black

This range will be sufficient for

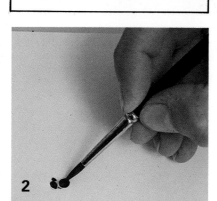

Left: *A selection of nibs to show the variety of lines that can be produced. The dip pen, which has a very wide range of nibs, may be most suitable for the beginner who is experimenting to find the pen and nib most suitable for his purposes. Choose your paper carefully; a heavy cartridge paper will provide the best surface, without absorbing too much of the ink.*

Left: *1. Using the edge of a piece of clean, wet blotting paper, soak up some of the ink from the blot as shown.*
2. If the paper is sufficiently strong to allow it, use a brush to apply clean water to the blot, then dab again with blotting paper.
3. Any stain remaining can be removed with a soft eraser.
4. If the eraser fails to remove all traces of the stain, you may be able to achieve the desired result with a scalpel. Be careful not to scratch through the paper! Afterwards, the surface of the paper should be smoothed down with a rounded object, like the back of a spoon.

1

2

3

4

almost all your needs. In addition you will require a palette which can be held while working, a selection of bristle brushes, turpentine for cleaning brushes and palette, and a clean rag. Try drawing with brushes, too, preferably sable, using either watercolour or ink.

Painting media Oil paint usually requires the addition of a medium to make the paint easier to apply and to thin down its consistency. Many media are available, most commonly a mixture of linseed oil and turpentine. Further thinning of the paint can be achieved by adding turpentine to the medium.

Surfaces Already stretched and prepared canvases are widely available and their natural springiness makes them the most pleasurable surface to work on. They are, however, relatively costly and a cheaper alternative is canvas board. Properly prepared, very thick cardboard can also be used, although it may lack permanence and will warp if not treated. Hardboard, prepared with special primer and sized on both sides so that it doesn't warp, is also adequate.

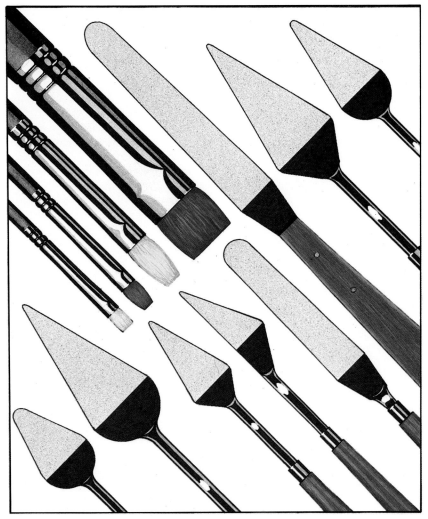

Above: *A selection of oil painting equipment. The three main brush shapes used for oil painting are bright, filbert and round, and you may also like to include a small sable as shown. Palette knives (two are shown with rounded blades) are essential for mixing paint. Painting knives are used to apply paint directly onto the canvas. For this purpose, they come in many shapes, with delicate blades.*

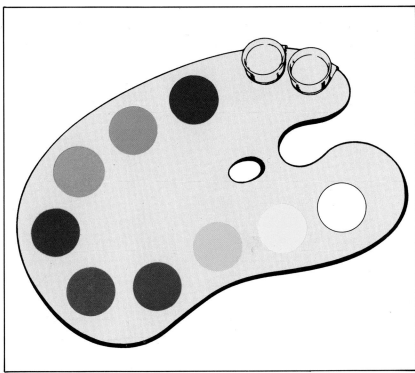

Left: *This is a very basic palette, containing the colours already suggested. You may like to substitute Lemon Yellow and Cadmium Yellow for Chrome Yellow, and to include Burnt Sienna and Ultramarine which will give you a greater flexibility when mixing dark colours.*

Making a mark

Before setting out to tackle any specific subject, it is very important that you have a working understanding of the widely differing properties and characteristics of the various materials available. You will probably, after having gained more experience, begin to establish your own preferences, but it is worth experimenting with as many as possible to begin with.

With pencils, practise varying the pressure in shading to learn control, and even when drawing a single line, to produce "accents" in its quality. Similarly, with charcoal or chalks, practise grading tones by rubbing and smudging the strokes with thumb or a rolled piece of paper. With any of these materials, experiment with various combinations, including lightly washed-in watercolour.

Tone can also be described using pen and ink, a purely line

Key:
1. F graphite pencil
2. HB graphite pencil
3. charcoal pencil
4. willow charcoal
5. 2B graphite pencil
6. 3B graphite pencil
7. red conté crayon
8. brown conté crayon
9. 6B graphite pencil
10. Wolff's carbon pencil
11. black conté crayon
12. pastel

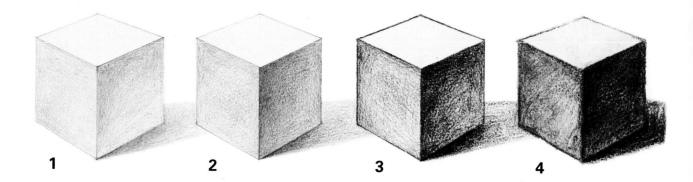

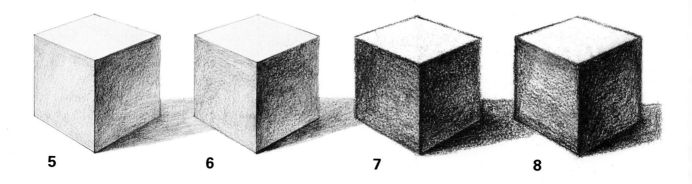

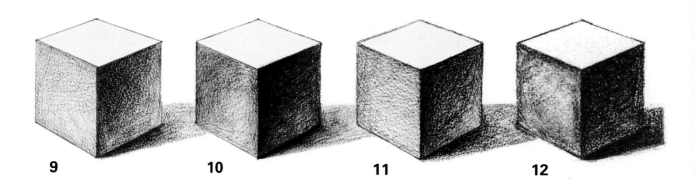

medium. This is suggested by "cross-hatching" and building up areas of delicate lines close together. A wide range of tones can be indicated by this method, especially when used in conjunction with watercolour washes. Do experiment with a variety of papers and background tints.

When using coloured pencils, try building up areas of colour by superimposing more than one colour as this will lend vitality to the finished result.

The diagrams of simple cubes on these pages show the variety and depth of tonal quality possible with the materials commonly associated with figure drawing. The F, HB, and 2B pencils, correctly sharpened, are admirable for crisp, incisive drawing. 3B to 6B are better suited to broader, quicker tonal work, while carbon pencils, charcoal, and conté produce a denser range without the unpleasant shine of lead instruments.

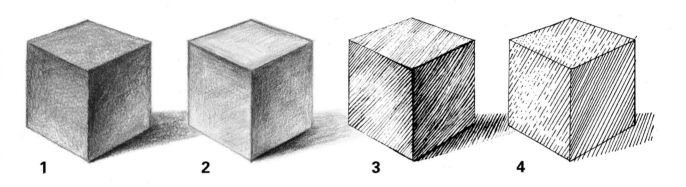

1   **2**   **3**   **4**

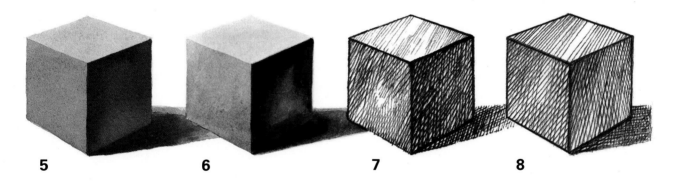

5   **6**   **7**   **8**

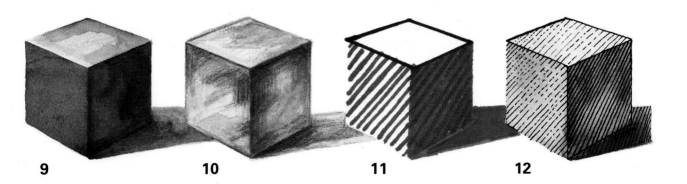

9   **10**   **11**   **12**

Learning to see

The act of drawing can be divided into two main areas: the intuitive and the analytical. The process of drawing involves a continual dialogue between the two, although the emphasis will depend on the type of drawing being made.

The process of perception

Light enters the eye reflected from the object and falls on the retina. The information is passed to the brain. The brain then instructs the hand to make certain marks, and evaluates those marks in relation to the subject, deciding if and how to correct them. This process is continued until the drawing is complete.

To start with, the act of drawing will be predominantly analytical, but as you gain experience and learn about colour, form, and texture, your intuitive or emotional response will show through more and more. In other words, you will acquire a visual language or vocabulary with which to guide the movements of hand and medium. The establishment of this vocabulary is absolutely essential if the artist is to bring order and clarity to his intuitive response. Without it, it is almost impossible for the artist to faithfully reflect creative attitudes to the subject he wishes to describe.

Optical illusion

Although our intuitive response to form is important for developing a feeling for the movement and angles of the figure, we need to consider consciously

Above: *The arrowheads have a misleading effect, making the line with outward-projecting arrowheads seem longer.*

the relationships between proportions and masses. Unless this is done, it is possible for our eyes to be misled, as in the diagram shown here where two lines of *equal* length appear to be unequal because of the effect of the arrowheads.

The cone of vision

The human eye has a "cone" of vision of about 60 degrees, i.e.,

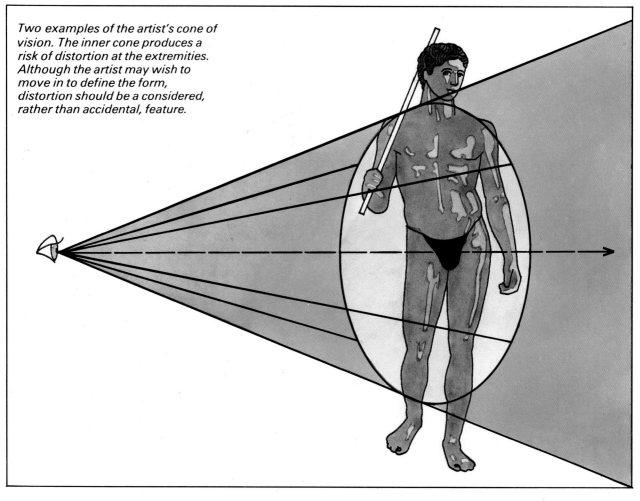

Two examples of the artist's cone of vision. The inner cone produces a risk of distortion at the extremities. Although the artist may wish to move in to define the form, distortion should be a considered, rather than accidental, feature.

about 30 degrees either side of the line of sight. Beyond this area distortions occur. Unless seeking a particular dramatic effect, it is best to position yourself no nearer than 6 feet from a seated figure and 10 feet from a standing one, in order to be able to take in the whole figure without moving your head.

To ascertain direction

A true vertical is best obtained with a plumbline and bob, or by setting up the drawing surface on the vertical plane and using the edge to give you a visual reference.

Compare any angle in the subject with an imaginary or actual vertical or horizontal before drawing it. For curves, it is useful to imagine a straight line running from one end of the curve to the other to help you assess the direction and degree of acuteness.

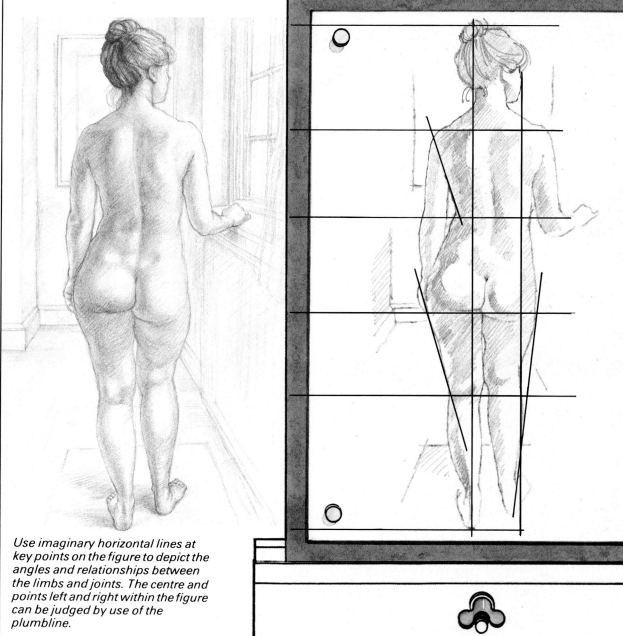

Use imaginary horizontal lines at key points on the figure to depict the angles and relationships between the limbs and joints. The centre and points left and right within the figure can be judged by use of the plumbline.

Aids to scale and proportion

Pencil measurements

Hold the pencil at arm's length toward the subject. Use the thumbnail to measure the apparent relative measurements from the pencil tip and transfer them to the paper. Provided that your arm remains straight, these measurements will all be proportionate. Never measure until you have already made a rough, intuitive sketch which can then be adjusted.

Distortion of scale

There tends to be a distortion of scale when drawing with the board resting on a "donkey" or chair, so a mental adjustment is necessary. When drawing on an easel, this will not be required as the drawing surface will be closer to eye level. If you are right-handed, look to the left of the easel so that the drawing hand and arm are not in the line of sight, and vice versa for left-handers. When using a chair or "donkey" keep the drawing board top clear of the subject.

Above: *Assessing scale by pencil measurement.*

Left: *With the board at an angle, a conscious adjustment must be made to avoid distortion. Always try to view the board at right angles.*

Exercises

1 – Scale and direction

Pin onto a wall or board random lengths of tape, wood strips or string up to about 4 feet long, stretched between thumbtacks. Concentrate on drawing as accurately as possible the lengths in relation to each other.

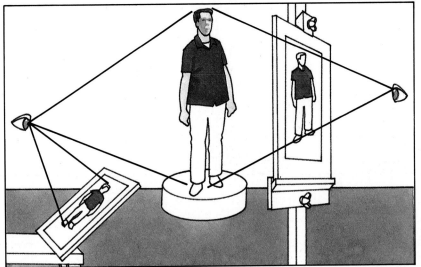

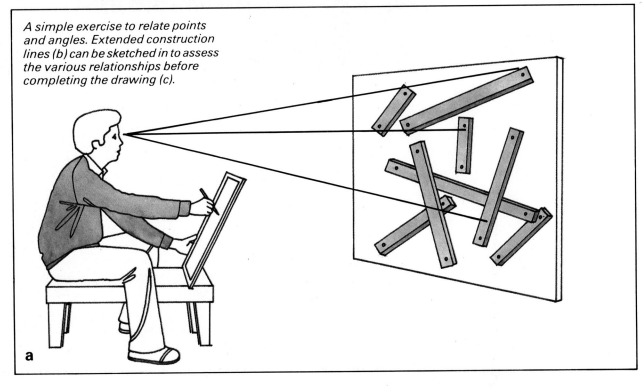

A simple exercise to relate points and angles. Extended construction lines (b) can be sketched in to assess the various relationships before completing the drawing (c).

a

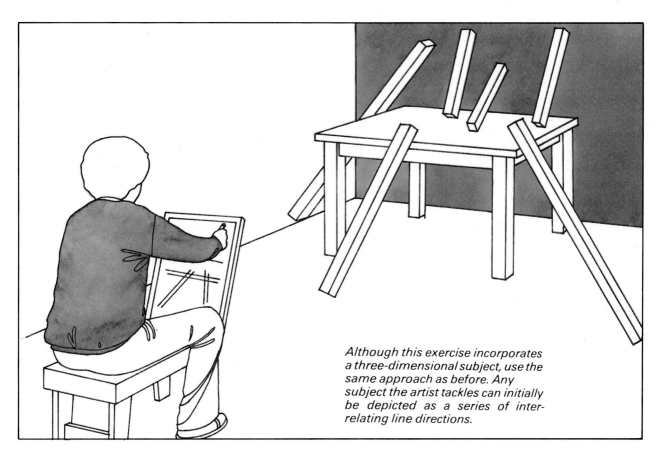

Although this exercise incorporates a three-dimensional subject, use the same approach as before. Any subject the artist tackles can initially be depicted as a series of inter-relating line directions.

2 – Proportions and angles

Place a table against a wall and arrange lengths of timber at random. Some will be sloping away from you and their proportions will be much harder to assess in a drawing. After drawing them intuitively, try to correct the drawing by using imaginary verticals and horizontals to relate the ends of each object in order to establish their positions in relation to each other. (Also see the example illustrated on page 15.)

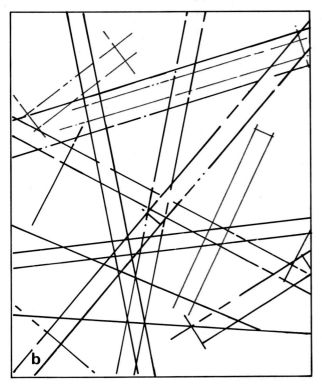

b

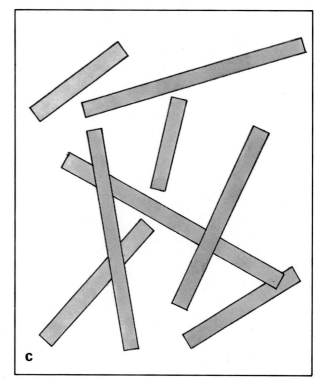

c

Perceiving form

It is an interesting fact that the mind always seeks to identify shapes as objects it knows. For example, the random line in figure 1 leaves a and b as empty areas, while the random line in figure 2 suggests the profile of a face and space d appears as a solid form.

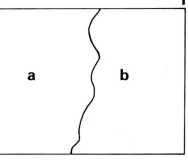

Negative shapes

When drawing the silhouette or flat shape of a figure on a blank, framed surface or picture plane, another shape is left between it and the outer edge. The figure we see as the positive shape, and the surrounding area as space. The consideration of both kinds of shape is of equal importance in drawing. In assessing the relationship between the shapes, both positive and negative should be viewed as being on the same plane and as flat areas bounded by qualities of line and tone, but without a sense of depth.

Paradoxically, the nature of the shapes seen on this "flat" plane will determine their position and scale in space. This thinking "flat," at various stages of the drawing, is essential for relating objects and figures to each other and for relating parts of the figure to the whole image. For example, if the standing figure has its hands on its hips, the space between the arm and the torso helps to relate the two parts accurately. So, too, in relating a seated figure to her chair, we must draw the shapes between the model's legs and the chair legs to correctly relate the model's legs to each other.

The third dimension

The outline/silhouette, or positive and negative shapes, are insufficient in themselves to recreate the three-dimensional aspect of the subject, as figure 3 indicates. The projection of the form can be shown as in figure 4, but even now it is difficult to decide whether we are seeing the boxes from above or below. In fact, we can read the forms

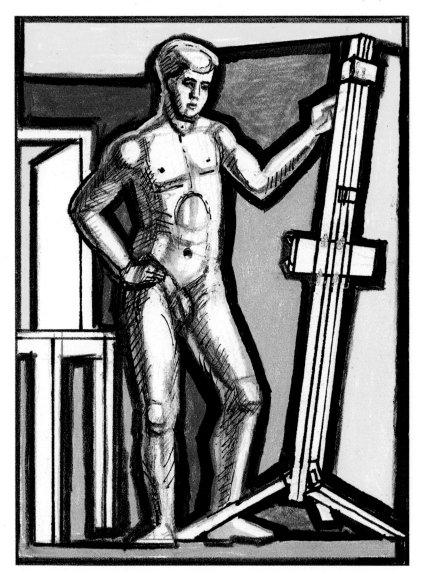

Left: *Three uses of negative shape are shown here: i) relating parts of the same object (the legs, the arms and head); ii) relating different objects such as the easel and model; iii) creating an interesting pictorial design between the main objects and the edge of the picture.*

Right: *The use of negative shape to indicate scale, as between the foreground and background figures.*

either way. By stressing the nearest planes of the boxes, using, for example, a thicker line, as in figure 5, we can decide that we are seeing them from a low eye level.

Finally, by observing two such boxes in this position more closely (figure 6), we see that the receding sides have their lines converging on an imaginary point and are not actually parallel. This is called perspective, and if observed correctly, it will remove all ambiguities.

When drawing a head and shoulders, as in figure 7, it will help to keep this solid-block construction in mind. In this diagram, the blocks are superimposed to show where the main "corners" or major changes of plane take place. Obviously, there are no hard lines or corners in the human figure, so we must work within this imaginary geometric shape, using tonal gradations or contour lines to show the real form.

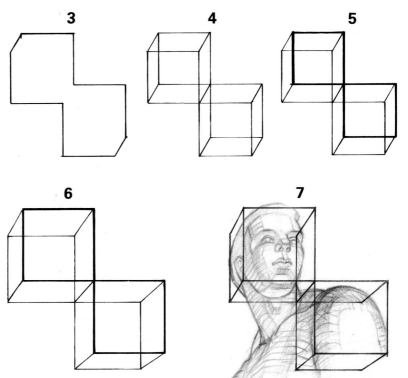

Anatomical structure

The basic anatomical factor in the human figure is the skeleton, which provides the support to which the muscles are attached. Whatever the size and weight of the muscle and fatty tissue on a figure, the artist must always be aware of the inner framework, or armature. The muscles can be considered as another mass built upon and around the inner skeleton.

The dynamics of movement and direction of muscle masses in space, the proportions of the figure and the muscles supported by the inner framework, all depend entirely on what the skeleton is doing.

Most important to the artist is the influence of the structure on the surface form of the figure. At certain points, the skeleton is very obvious and its hardness provides a useful contrast to the more fleshy areas. Bony areas are to be found on the head and face, where the skull is all-important, and at the knee, ankle, wrist, shoulder, elbow, foot, and hand.

The illustrations on these pages show the main bones of the skeleton (below) *and skull* (near right). *The main muscles, which power the movement of the "ball and socket" and "hinge" lever system of the bones of the skeleton, are shown* below right *and* far right.

Key (the skeleton):
 1. Skull
 2. Clavicle
 3. Rib cage
 4. Sternum
 5. Humerus
 6. Spinal column
 7. Radius
 8. Ulna
 9. Pelvis
10. Great trochanter
11. Carpals
12. Metacarpals
13. Phalanges
14. Femur
15. Patella
16. Tibia
17. Fibula
18. Calcaneus
19. Tarsals
20. Metatarsals
21. Phalanges
22. Frontal bone
23. Parietal bone
24. Temporal bone
25. Occipital bone
26. Zygoma
27. Maxilla
28. Mandible
29. Scapula
30. Seven cervical vertebrae
31. Twelve dorsal vertebrae
32. Five lumbar vertebrae
33. Sacrum and coccyx
Opposite, above:
34. Parietal bone
35. Frontal bone
36. Orbit
37. Nasal
38. Malar
39. Maxilla
40. Mandible
41. Zygoma
42. Temporal bone

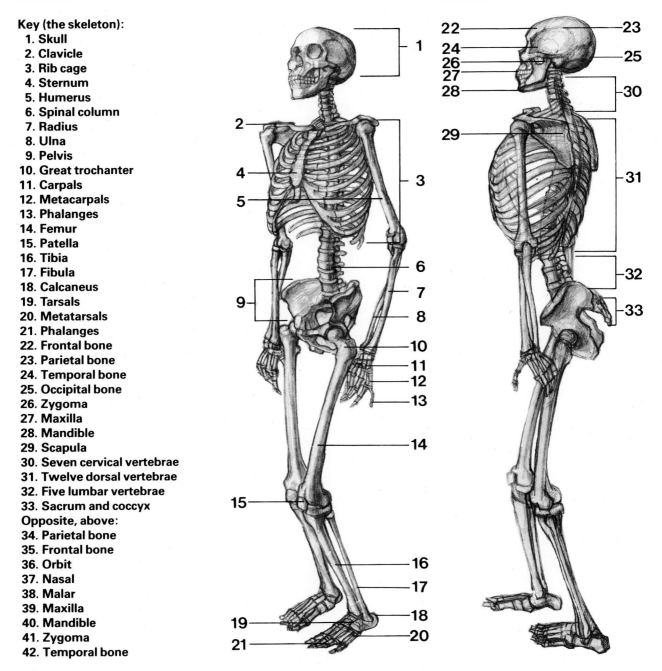

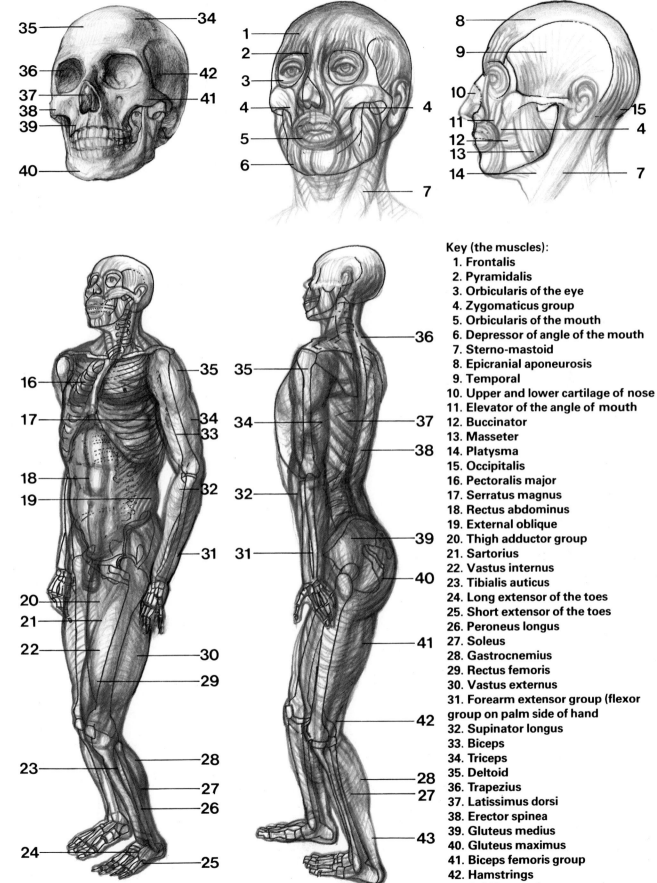

Key (the muscles):
1. Frontalis
2. Pyramidalis
3. Orbicularis of the eye
4. Zygomaticus group
5. Orbicularis of the mouth
6. Depressor of angle of the mouth
7. Sterno-mastoid
8. Epicranial aponeurosis
9. Temporal
10. Upper and lower cartilage of nose
11. Elevator of the angle of mouth
12. Buccinator
13. Masseter
14. Platysma
15. Occipitalis
16. Pectoralis major
17. Serratus magnus
18. Rectus abdominus
19. External oblique
20. Thigh adductor group
21. Sartorius
22. Vastus internus
23. Tibialis auticus
24. Long extensor of the toes
25. Short extensor of the toes
26. Peroneus longus
27. Soleus
28. Gastrocnemius
29. Rectus femoris
30. Vastus externus
31. Forearm extensor group (flexor group on palm side of hand
32. Supinator longus
33. Biceps
34. Triceps
35. Deltoid
36. Trapezius
37. Latissimus dorsi
38. Erector spinea
39. Gluteus medius
40. Gluteus maximus
41. Biceps femoris group
42. Hamstrings
43. Achilles tendon

Analyzing movement

Even in a static subject like a still-life there can be as much "movement" as in a drawing of a galloping horse. True pictorial movement, as opposed to literal movement, is due to the interplay between directional lines, suggesting angles and curves between salient points. These directional lines can be either actual or implied, and this applies as much to a seated or standing figure as to one which is running or walking.

The composition created by the relationship of these main directional lines of figure and background alters as we walk around the model in search of a suitable drawing position, and should influence our eventual choice. Without a strong, exciting design, created by these lines, the figure drawing will lack vitality, however much detail is put into the finished image.

Finding a direction

Always look for the main directions of the pose, as indicated by the torso, head, and limbs, before concentrating on details. A poor composition, however accurate in execution, will not present the figure as a convincing whole.

The main directions in the figure are not necessarily the outlines, but are often imaginary lines or axial directions of the skeleton running through the middle of the outward forms. The construction lines produce the vital "push-and-pull" effect of the forms in space. They often begin and end at the joints of the skeleton.

Although these directions must be "felt" intuitively at first, we can check for accuracy later with pencil and plumbline as described earlier. Indeed, as the drawing progresses, the linking of points by extending these construction lines horizontally, vertically, and diagonally can create lines of reference on which the entire figure is to be based. For example, a line of gravity identified in a standing figure running vertically from head to ankle will help in assessing other directions.

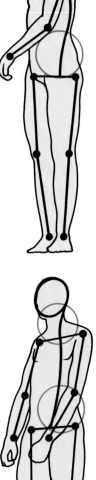

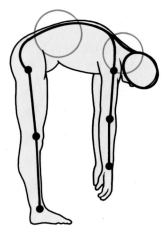

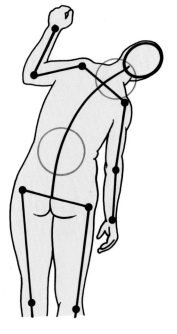

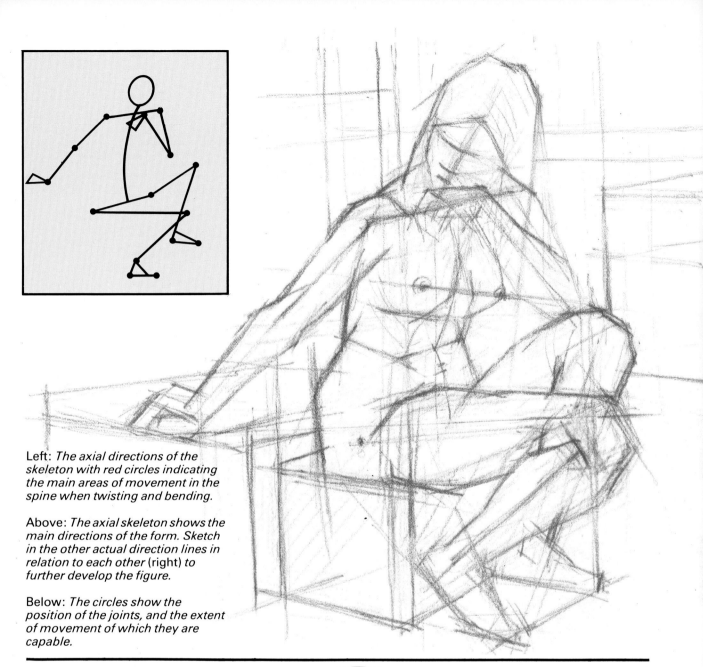

Left: *The axial directions of the skeleton with red circles indicating the main areas of movement in the spine when twisting and bending.*

Above: *The axial skeleton shows the main directions of the form. Sketch in the other actual direction lines in relation to each other (right) to further develop the figure.*

Below: *The circles show the position of the joints, and the extent of movement of which they are capable.*

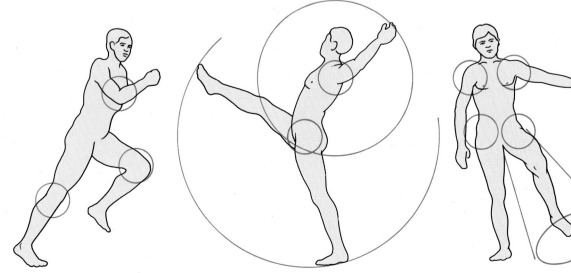

Constructing form

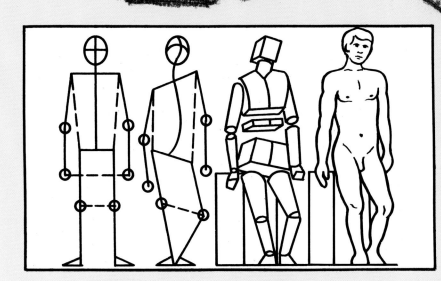

Before developing detail and subtlety of form, we must learn to think of the figure as a series of solid volumes which can move in relation to one another. The underlying forms of these volumes can be viewed as simple blocks based on the cube, cylinder, or sphere. Artists throughout history have based their initial visual consideration of a figure on this principle.

The most important blocks or masses are the upper and lower thorax (rib cage and pelvic girdle), which govern the position and direction of the blocks

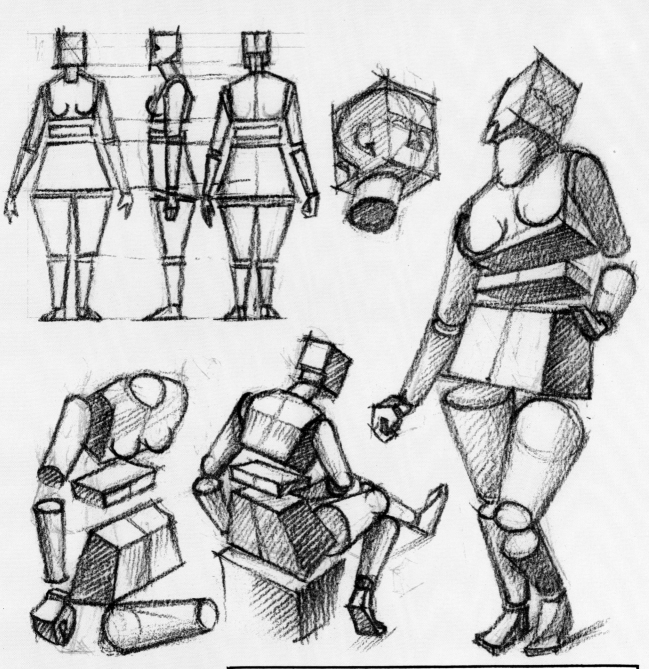

representing the head, neck, and limbs. It is useful to practise bending and twisting these blocks, bearing in mind the drawings on the previous page. In this way, the figure will reveal itself as being solid from the outset, and this conception of the figure as a series of simple masses is invaluable in constructing imaginary figures seen from different eye levels and viewpoints.

There are obvious differences in proportions of height, width, and mass between male and female forms as shown here.

Using line

If we draw an outline of a disk viewed from above, we produce a circle as in figure 1, but as we look at the disk from various eye levels as a series of side views, we see that the shapes become ellipses as in figure 2. By strengthening the line of the edge of the disk that is nearest to us, we can "read" more successfully whether the disk is above or below our eye level.

Describing solid form

If we wish to represent solid form with line, then we have to make our line express other things besides just outline shape. By projecting the ellipses onto the circle, we can see that solid form is made up of horizontal and vertical sections through the circle (figure 3).

Now imagine the outline shape of a section through the human head (or what we would see as the silhouette of a shadow cast on a wall), as in figure 4. Keeping this same section of the head in mind, turn the head around until it is in a three-quarter position as in figure 5, and the edge of the imaginary section would form a line down the front centre of the head, over the top and down the opposite side. This would now reflect the form or "terrain" of the head as seen from a perspective viewpoint. This line, and particularly the part of it following the undulating form of the face, is called a *contour*.

Sections can also be imagined as though cut horizontally through the form (figures 6 and 7), and it is very important to be aware of the form right through and around the back and not just in the visible portion of the figure. This technique helps us to understand, and therefore express accurately, the whole solid form through a network of contour lines. Even when drawing from a single viewpoint, it is important to view the model from other positions to understand the form "in the round."

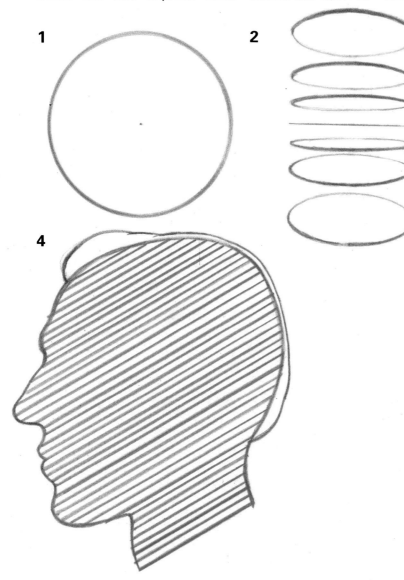

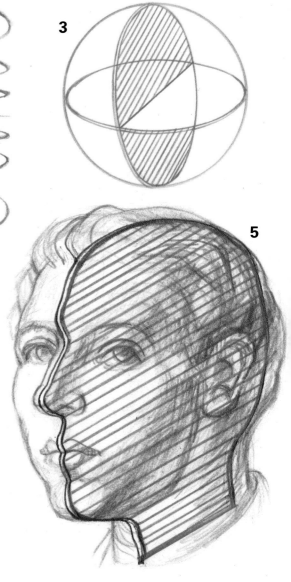

6

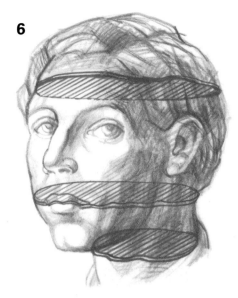

7

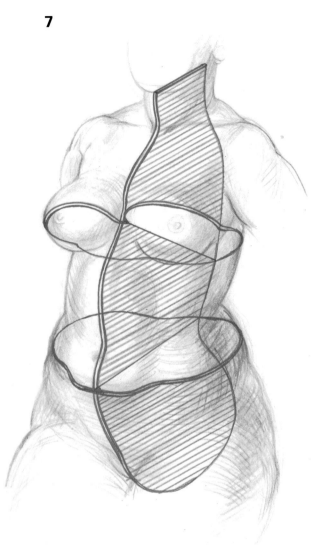

Understanding symmetry

With symmetrical forms like the human head, the outline of a cheek bone or temple is directly opposite the other in perspective, which, although not seen as outline, must be expressed as contour. Even if the other portion is not actually drawn, it must be imagined in the correct position. This accurate placing applies to the corners of the eyes, nostrils, and mouth (figure 8). An imaginary centre contour line running down the head is vital, and a series of section lines

8

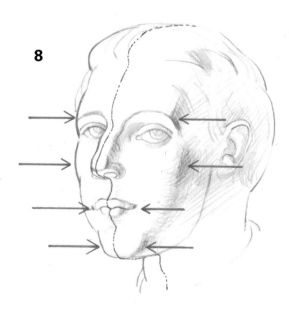

9

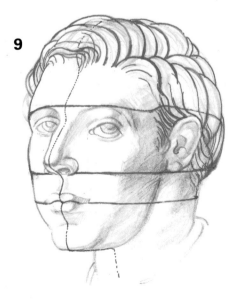

across the head will help considerably. In a line drawing, the main lines of the hair growth can act as contour lines describing the form (figure 9, page 27).

Contours and volume

When viewing a cylindrical form as in figure 1, the vertical outlines should describe the points on either side where the curving surface disappears behind the mass. This point is shown clearly by drawing the elliptical section and the lines of sight running from the artist's eye to the very edge of the cylinder.

When our eye level is halfway between the top and the bottom (figure 2), we can only describe the ends of the cylinder by curved lines indicating the near edges of the cylinder top and bottom before the surface curves out of sight. Great care must be taken, therefore, to observe exactly where this turning away takes place. The effectiveness of the drawn outline and contour depends on how well we observe the section or "turn" of the form from its nearest point to us and should give the feeling of continuing around behind the form.

Assessing the human form

The volumes of the figure are rarely, if ever, perfectly circular or cylindrical. They range from nearly boxlike to ovoid or nearly circular. For example, if we feel the section of our own wrists, we will feel that it is a flattened, boxlike form compared with a rounder ovoid form further up the lower arm. It is wrong to use circular contour lines unless representative of the form.

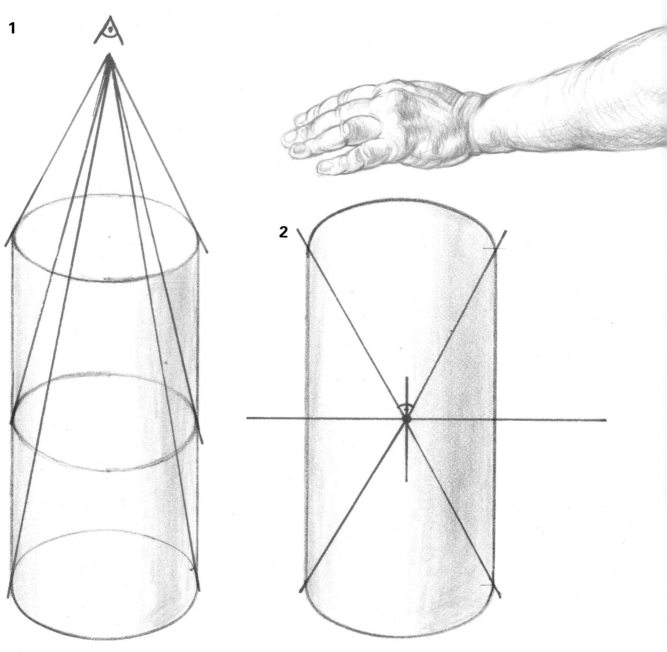

1

2

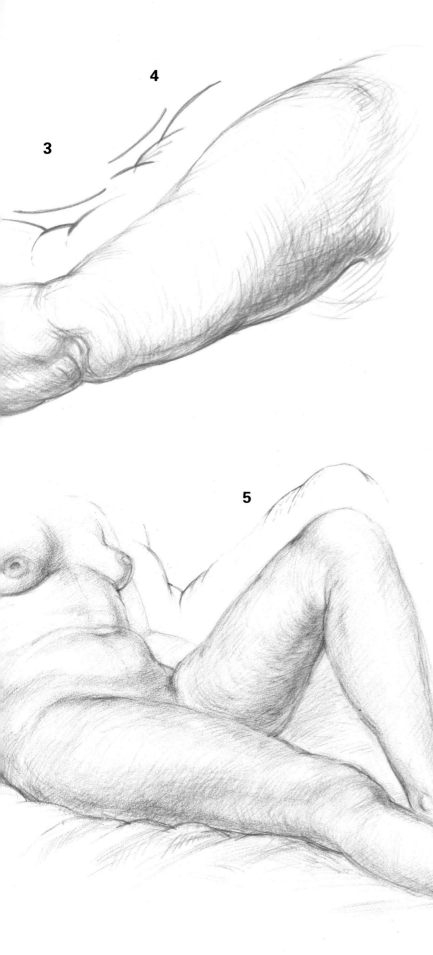

4

3

5

The forms of the figure overlap and twist around the bone and are convex in nature, even when the forms are small, as in our fingers and toes. What often appears to be a concave line at the edge of a figure is, on closer examination, a series of subtle overlappings of convex forms as in figures 3, 4, and 5.

Contours overlap around the form and, if drawn well, give the feeling of "going around the back of the figure." The contour originates from the outline but turns inwards, however subtly, onto the form and curves round the volume of the figure. Wrinkles or creases are natural contour lines describing form, but are seldom sufficient by themselves.

The technique by which we express the form is secondary to what it is that needs to be expressed, i.e., in what direction the form is going in relation to the artist and to other forms, and what its physical character is as a mass.

The contours used to express the turn of the form around the axis of a limb or torso, and its direction in space relative to the artist, are related to expression of the nature of the form.

Above and left: *In the diagrams 3, 4 and 5, some of the contours of the finished figure are represented in a slightly exaggerated form. If the drawing is completed tonally, the lines used to express these contours may be emphasized by shaded areas, which will give a feeling of volume in the drawing.*

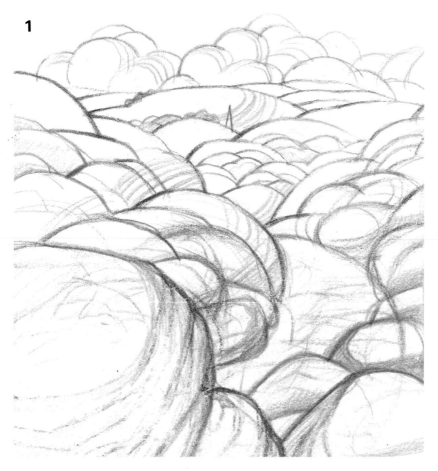

Contour drawing

The main directions of the volumes in the drawing below are shown by the accompanying diagrams of sections through the form. Many forms are partly hidden from view by those in front, so think of the contours going behind and being over-lapped by those in front, as we would draw a distant range of hills in a landscape. See figures 1 and 2. It will help to think of the shape of the human figure as being analogous to the terrain of a landscape.

The contours used in expres-sing the turn of the form should be drawn with reference to the light and dark areas as the form turns to and from the light source. The contours will appear

Left: *The full, rich forms of rocks, hills and clouds are expressed by overlapping contours in a landscape drawing.*

Below: *In reality, the contours of the nude figure are much more subtle than in the diagram opposite.*

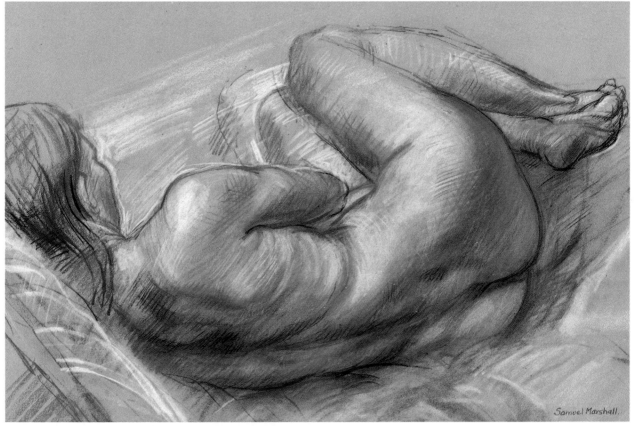

Samuel Marshall.

darker as they curve away from the light, but a complete tonal rendition should be left to a drawing in charcoal, chalk, or paint. Contour drawings select from the whole range of tones only those which are needed to "turn" and describe the form. Very often the darkest tone is not the edge of the form but where the major plane of the front turns around to the side plane.

Contour drawing can become a very personal visual language, differing from artist to artist. The lines in a Dürer engraving, for example, are very different from those in the pen drawings of Rubens, Michaelangelo, or Raphael. It is worth making accurate copies of some of these with a view to understanding the artist's use of line.

2

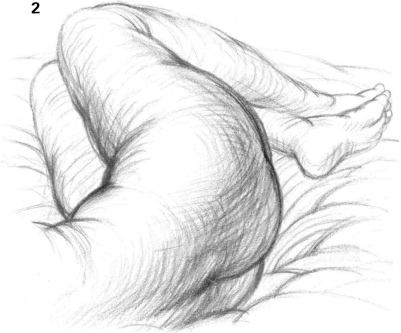

Above right: *The human figure can be expressed by overlapping contours, as in landscape forms.*

Below: *Varying sections, with contour lines and showing the axial direction, through parts selected from the drawing opposite.*

Right: *This shows the difference between outline and contour in expressing sections through form. In a) the outline does not convey the volume or direction of the bottle. In b) the label acts as a contour, explaining both the section through volume and the direction.*

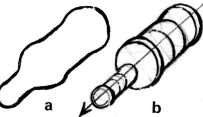

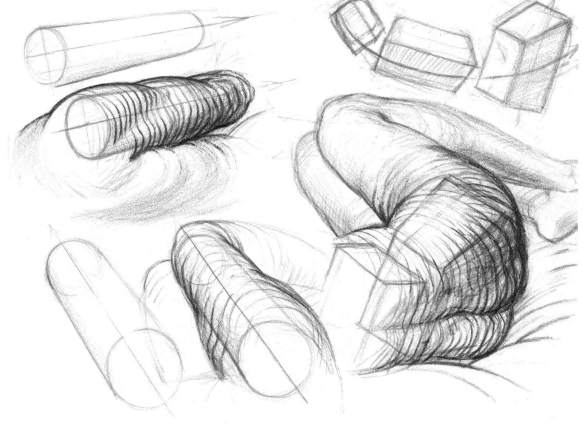

31

Tonal drawing

In relying totally on line to express volume or mass, the artist limits himself. For example, if we attempt to describe a sphere by outline alone, as in figure 1, it can easily be mistaken for a hoop. If we look at a sphere, we see that the turning surfaces reflect varying degrees of light. If we look at a cube (figures 2 and 3), we see that the same applies to its various surfaces. If we understand the simple logic behind light and dark, we can express all these volumes far more convincingly.

In representing volumes, as in figures 3 to 6, the artist must select from nature the tones that will explain the turn of the form most effectively. When explaining structure, the artist can leave out any shadows that distort the form. He must be selective rather than photographic if he is to express the three-dimensional nature of his subject.

Light and form

The basic principle behind defining volume by use of tone begins with the direction of the light falling on the surfaces. The object divides itself into two main areas: those planes receiving varying degrees of direct light and those which are in

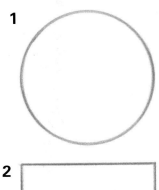

1

2

3

4

Right: *When dealing with areas of light and dark in portrait drawing, first lightly sketch in the proportions of the head and features, then immediately model in tone, using the side of the pencil and keeping the tonal areas broad. Gradually cross-hatch with the point of the pencil to deepen and define the tones and contour lines as indicated on the previous page.*

7

shadow. The tones in the light areas grade from light to "halftones" and the shadows should also vary in density to explain the form. These variations are called *reflected lights,* being reflected from a nearby surface, and help to illuminate the form in areas which might otherwise be a flat, dark shadow. The deepest dark is often found where the form changes direction most abruptly. The shadow that is seen on the horizontal surface on which the object rests is thrown by the object itself, and also helps to explain form. It should not be reproduced too densely or it will compete with the form rather than support it.

Tone in people

Many fine figure drawings do not contain deep shadow tones, the artist using the minimum range necessary to explain the structure, often lighting his model from the front so that even the plane furthest away is only a halftone, the shadow areas being around the back. This is illustrated in figure 6.

In figure 7, the head is lit from the model's right. The major planes are the side, front, and top of the head, and all the features are minor forms within the main one on which they are situated. For example, the "wedge" form of the nose and

the sockets of the eyes are drawn, tonally, in relation to the main planes of the face and forehead, which are seen as a strong contrast to the light background. The ear is part of the light side plane and should not be drawn too dark.

In figure 8, the main light is coming from the model's left. Again the face is not fully lit but is in shadow. The modelling of the features is by reflected lights and the face merges into a strong cast shadow on the wall, instead of being clearly defined.

Notice that the hair and clothing receive the same light and are drawn with reference to the form beneath.

5

6

Right: *When indicating tone in the background, in order to preserve a feeling of the volume of the head it is sometimes necessary to play down the depth of background tone, even if very dark. This is particularly so if a dark background tone delineates the edge of the face very sharply, as this can destroy the feeling of space around the head.*

8

Light and dark masses

When drawing in tone, it is important to see your subject as an arrangement of light and dark masses, and not as a line drawn around the figure which is later "filled in." Have the courage to put down the masses as broadly as possible from the beginning. Try half closing your eyes before starting to draw in order to eliminate the unimportant details and help you see the positions of the main light and dark masses.

Drawing is relating the line, tone, and mass of the whole subject. This is helped tonally by seeing the design or composition of the light and dark areas as a flat, interacting pattern. Though we may be stressing

volume, this appreciation of the pattern created is important in even the quickest drawing. It helps us to see the placing of the main volumes in relation to each other more accurately. Try to make use of the cast shadows around the figure, however light, to help show the figures's relationship to the floor, wall, chair, etc. Any contours should be drawn with reference to the arrangement of light and dark.

A drawing can also be a complete study of the tonal relationship between figure and background, where every colour area in your subject is considered as a tone of light or dark within the chosen tonal range. This is known as a "scale" of tonal values. The range of tones can

vary from subject to subject; in some the scale ranges from light to very dark and in others from light to soft greys.

Again, the design or composition of pattern of these tonal areas is very important, particularly in a preparatory drawing or a monochrome study for a painting.

Below: *This figure was drawn swiftly with soft conté crayon, the main inspiration being the inter-relating volumes which were expressed tonally.*

Right: *Here the pictorial design of lights and darks is important. Establish two or three areas of light and dark broadly at first and work into each tone to achieve intermediate tones.*

Samuel Marshall.

34

Marshall

Proportion

In observing people around us, we see a great variety of differences in figure proportions, and this variety is important to the accuracy of a drawing. There is, however, a fairly widely accepted "norm" or average from which deviations such as "fat" or "thin" occur. This standard will be only a basic guide, but it does give the artist some point of reference for assessing more individual figures.

The drawings on this page show how the figure can be described by a circle, and by a triangle. This is apparent when we look at a figure from an undistorted viewpoint.

However, many viewpoints involve foreshortening of the head, torso, limbs, and the actual observed proportions of the body are seen to change radically.

When faced with this problem, it is important to remember that we are drawing a normal human figure and that the

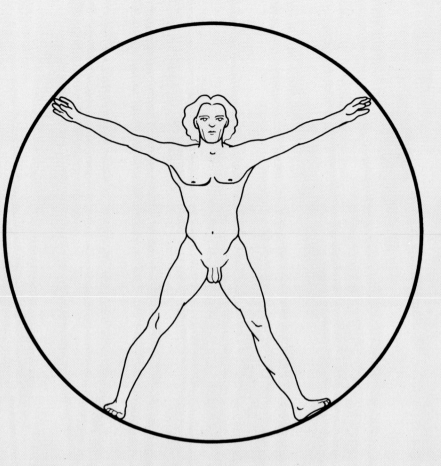

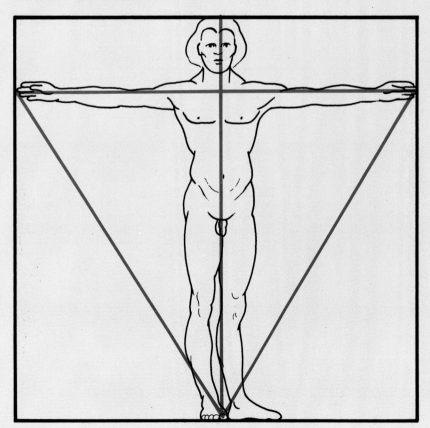

Above and left: *These illustrations are based on Leonardo da Vinci's theories of proportion and represent ideals which may be considered a synthesis of many differing proportions. They are useful as a starting point from which to observe the variety of ways in which individuals differ.*

distortions are not deformities. Foreshortening is a product of perspective and will affect the box-structure of the masses that describe the figure.

Proportions of the head

The side view of the head, from the top of the skull to the chin and from the tip of the nose to the back of the skull, is basically a square. The total width across the skull goes into the total height about one and a half times. The hair is an extra layer or mass on top of this.

The head, even in the smoother female form, should

be shown to have a front, side, top, bottom, and back plane. A vertical line down the middle may be used, and horizontal proportion lines for the features should be placed at one-third intervals: the first placed at the level of the line of the eyebrows, the second on a level with the base of the nose.

The top of the ear is level with the eyebrows and the bottom with the nostril. The mouth is halfway between the chin and nose and the eyes are an eye-width apart. These proportions describe the standard adult. Children have smaller faces in proportion to their skulls.

Right: *These two diagrams show how perspective alters our perception of a box and a figure and provides an elementary aid to drawing foreshortened or "end-on" subjects.*

Below: *When drawing a face or head, it is essential to fix the basic proportions first. These are the height and the width, and from here they can be broken down as shown below. Here the main features divide the face up into thirds but remember that the proportions will alter visually from different viewpoints.*

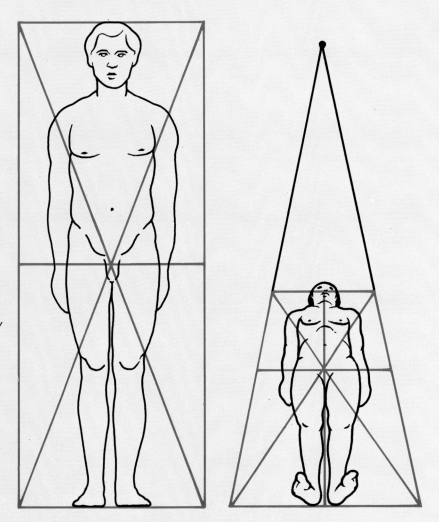

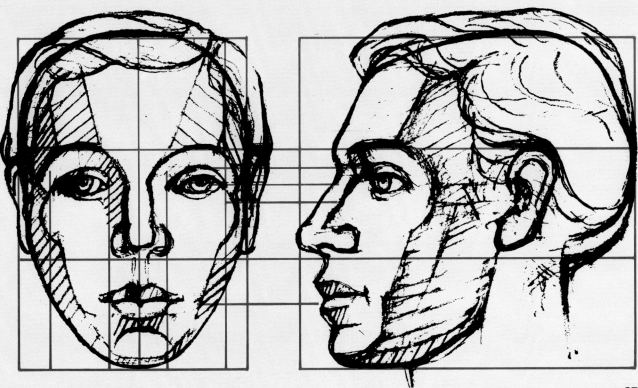

Analysis of proportion

In the normal male figure, the halfway point is near the base of the trunk, level with the trochanter. The kneecap is halfway between the centre and the soles of the feet. The waist and shoulders fall approximately at one-third intervals between the top of the head and the base of the trunk, but, in the male figure, the lower third is usually smaller to allow for the larger thorax. The limbs, hands, and feet are also usually larger than in the female.

The male's shoulders can be thought of as being two head-lengths wide, and are usually wider than the hips and more square than the female's. The bone and muscle structure in the male are usually very evident in the angularity of the forms. The head is boxlike in structure, with the skull somewhat larger and heavier than in the female, and the figure is usually eight head-lengths high.

Right and opposite: Fix the greatest overall dimension first, then make the largest divisions possible both vertically and horizontally. Repeat the process down to the smallest areas, as shown.

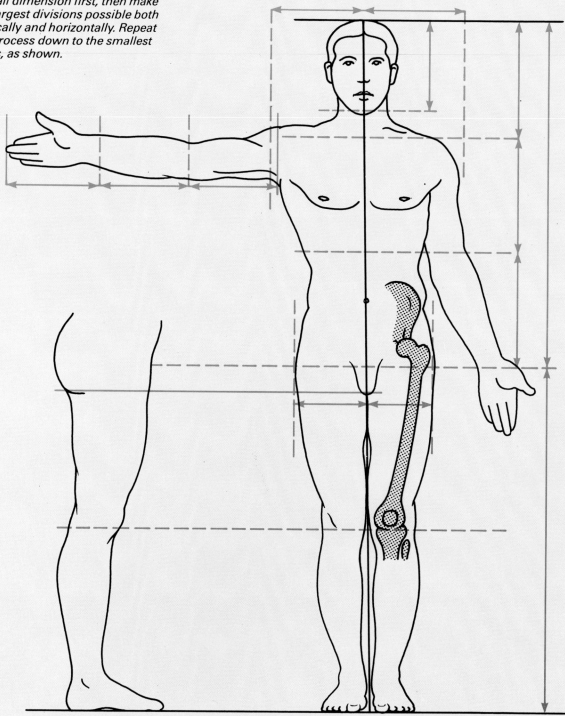

In the female figure the half-way point is in the middle of the trochanter. The middle third, or upper thorax, of the upper half is usually smaller than the male's, and can be described by lowering and sloping the line of the shoulders and raising the waistline. The female figure differs from the male chiefly in the relative widths of shoulders and hips. The pelvis is usually wider and the shoulders narrower.

The head is slightly smaller and more oval and the planes and structure of the figure are rounder and smoother due to the presence of fatty tissue in certain areas. For example, the flank seems to extend as one mass into the buttocks, and this gives the lower thorax or pelvis a characteristic form. The width of the pelvis increases the outward angle of the thigh bone from the knee to the trochanter, and the width of the thigh at and just below the trochanter to the lower third of the thigh is also a characteristic in the female.

Always work from large to small areas and check your proportions after you have intuitively drawn them. This will develop your judgement and imbue the finished drawing with greater vitality.

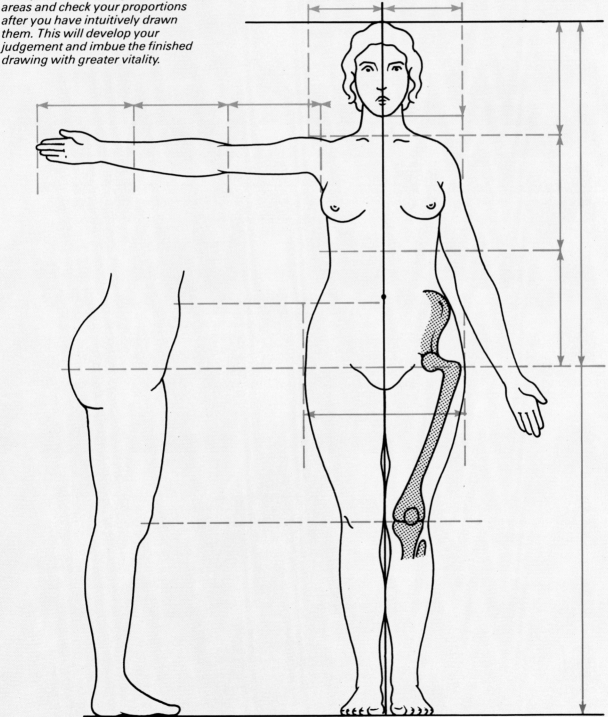

Children: proportions

When drawing figures it is important to understand the variations from the "norm" that occur at the various stages of human growth and aging. If these are seen and drawn correctly, the figure will accurately represent the age of the subject.

During the first twenty years of life, there are more proportional changes in the human figure than at any other time (see figure 1). The length of the

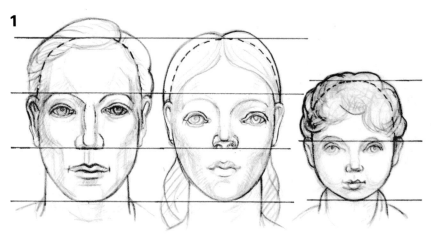

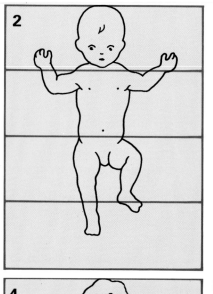

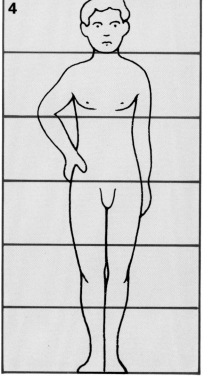

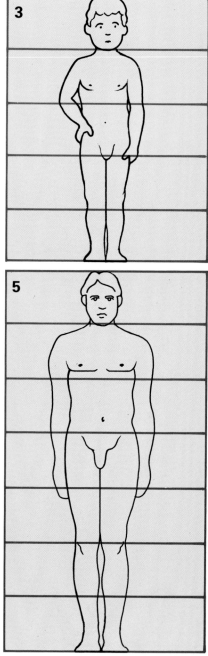

new-born baby's head is about half that of the adult and is not as long proportionally, being squarer. The face, however, is very small due to the undeveloped skeleton, and the centre of the head therefore lies above the eyes in the baby instead of level with them. The head grows more in length than in breadth.

The mid-point of the body is above the navel and drops with growth. The infant trunk is very prominent and the limbs are proportionally short, with the upper limbs longer than the lower at first. By about seven years, the limbs are equal, and gradually the length of the legs exceeds that of the arms. At ten years, the foot is the same length as the head. Before that it is shorter and after that longer. A table of typical body lengths would be: one year – 4 head lengths (figure 2); four years – 5 head lengths (figure 3); nine years – 6 head lengths (figure 4); fifteen years – 7 head lengths (figure 5).

The elderly: proportions

While the general proportions of the skeleton remain the same in old age, the regression of the muscle masses alters the adult figure. Shrinking of these masses takes place and more emphasis is placed on the skeletal form. Because of the reduction in muscular strength, the height of the figure is diminished as the elderly figure stoops. The head is thrown forwards and downwards and the chest area declines toward the abdomen. The legs become bent at the knees as the muscles relax.

Regressive changes also take place in the structure of the head in old age. Teeth are lost, with the result that the dental margins are reduced. The form of the facial planes are affected too. The lips tend to curl back into the mouth and the angle of the lower jaw opens out to about 140 degrees. The shape of the skull reasserts itself and has a pronounced influence on the form as the flesh of the face becomes shrunken. The feet lose their springiness and arch, the person moving with a flat, shuffling gait.

Right: *Regressive changes of aging.*

Below: *This drawing shows how observed proportions alter in a reclining pose. The vertical and horizontal lines serve two purposes i) to describe the varying areas (e.g. the space taken up by the leg in relation to the torso) and ii) help to place the points (e.g. along the line from hip to chin).*

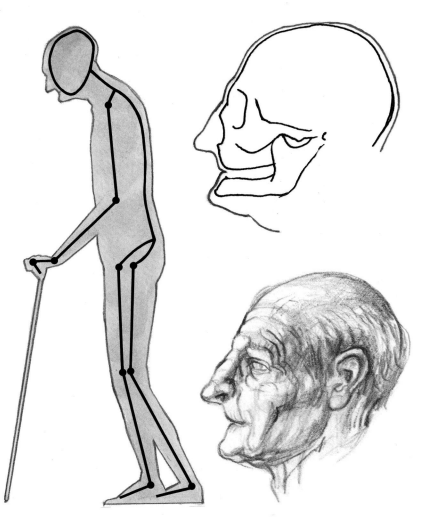

Samuel Marshall.

Recording detail

The masses, or block forms, of the hands and feet are governed by the bone structure.

Hands

In the hand, apart from the rounder masses of the ball of the thumb and the palm, the planes are angular and well defined. Construction lines should be used to help locate the key points.

The block-line form of the lower arm joins the bones of wrist and palm which make one important block with a clearly defined plane, i.e., the back of the hand which is large and slightly convex. A small plane runs down the outside to the first joint of the little finger. On the thumb side there is a larger, wedge-shaped plane.

The line of the knuckles is extremely important, as they define the major changes of the planes of the fingers. The bones of the fingers are squarish in section, particularly at the knuckles.

Below: *Many people are convinced that a hand is too difficult to draw; it may help to think of it in terms of a form or block.*

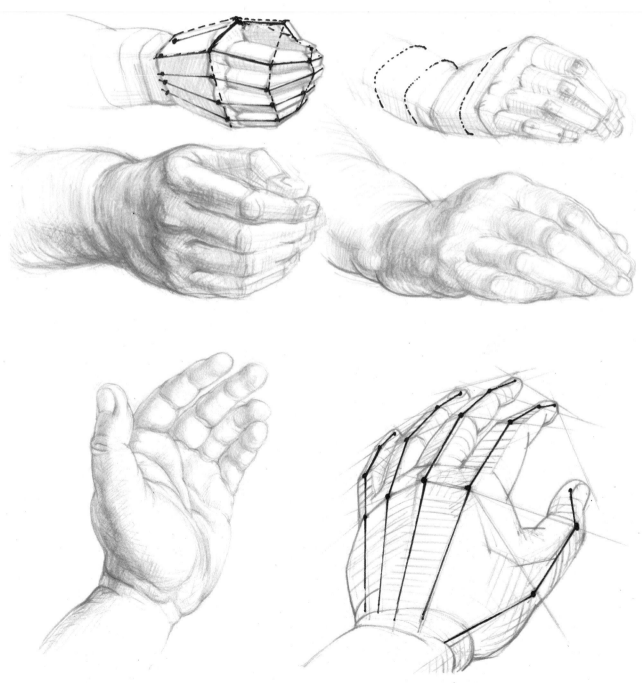

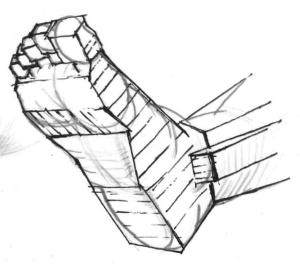

Left: *Look at the skeleton to establish the inner axial direction of the bones, as the form of the foot is governed by its bone structure.*

Below: *Feet and hands can both be considered as miniature "landscapes" of planes and forms. From the block form you must then evolve a more rounded and flowing natural line. Also consider the form of the foot when extended.*

Feet

In drawing the foot, as with the hand, the bone structure has a very obvious influence on the block form. In contrast to the wrist, the comparable bone mass in the foot, the tarsals, meets the shaft of the ankle at right angles where they fit into a joint, as in the wrist and lower arm, and allow for considerable movement. The inner joint of the ankle is higher than the outer and this influences the outward and downward tilt of the top plane of the instep towards the toes. The high ridge running down to the big toe marks the major change of plane from top to side plane.

The inner-side plane then curves underneath to allow for the arch of the foot between the squarish mass of the heel and the ball of the foot at the toe end. The toes themselves are smaller, squarish blocks, starting with the larger mass of the big toe and diminishing to the little toe. The latter also marks the end of the important bevel or outside plane of the foot, just as the little finger marks that of the hand. Again, use construction lines to establish main points, remembering that, like the hand, the foot can be flexed or extended.

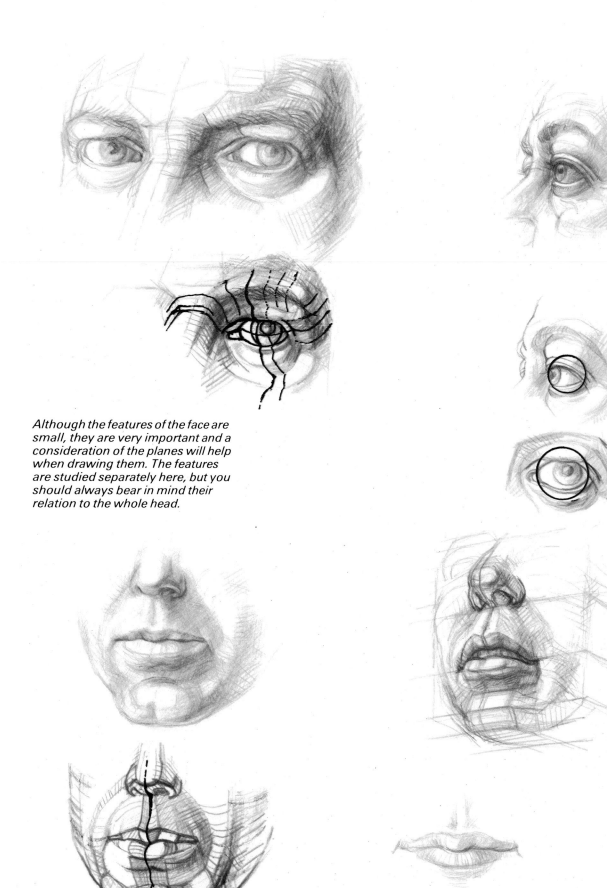

Although the features of the face are small, they are very important and a consideration of the planes will help when drawing them. The features are studied separately here, but you should always bear in mind their relation to the whole head.

Eyes

The eye is a ball set into a socket or recess in the front of the face. The beginning of the top plane of the socket is marked by the eyebrows, and the inside plane is a continuation of the upper-side plane of the nose. The outside and lower planes are the projections of the cheekbones. The upper eyelid slides up and down over the eyeball, while the lower one remains almost stationary.

Lips

The fullness of the lips projecting from the front plane of the face is governed to some degree by the curvature of the teeth behind them. The upper lip starts below the nose with a small groove or wedge-shaped centre, flanked by planes tapering to the corners of the mouth. The lower lip overhangs a plane sloping back to the ball of the chin, and the surface divides into two rounded forms that meet in a slight depression. In most cases, the lower lip is fuller than the upper lip.

Nose

The basic form of the nose is a wedge-shaped mass arising from the frontal plane of the face. Its front plane starts just under the forehead and separates the two eye sockets. The top part is narrow and bony; the lower part is cartilage and forms the central "bulb" between the two nostrils. The latter, though curved, lie on the two wedge-shaped side planes and their bases form a flat plane.

Ears

The ears tend to slant inwards and downwards, parallel to the cheeks, and can be divided into thirds from top to bottom. The centre is the "bowl," the lower third is the lobe, and the upper is the curling rim of the ear. These forms, although small, are fully modelled and twisting in character, not flat. The back view shows a shallow "trumpet." The ear and nose are on a level and are the same depth.

Hair

It is important to regard hair also as a mass. Although its soft texture and our awareness that it is composed of separate strands makes this difficult, the hair should be thought of as an extra layer over the skull. Sometimes the hair lies very close to the skull and accentuates the form, while at other times, though lying close to the skull at the top, it can break away to form block forms of its own. The linear movement of the growth of hair within the mass should help to describe the form.

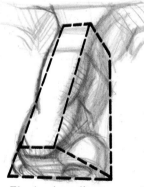

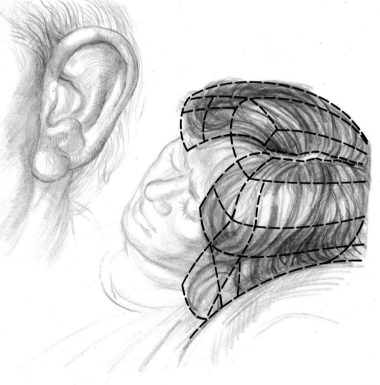

Above: *The broken diagrammatic lines on the nose show the underlying essential wedge-block form on which the more subtle forms are built.*

Right: *When drawing hair, try to avoid superficially copying its appearance. Use the basic planes shown here so that the natural movement of the hair can be represented.*

Tackling a subject

The drawings reproduced in the next few pages contain many of the factors discussed so far. The illustrations will examine these factors in more detail.

Figure 1 illustrates the position and direction of movement of the main axial-skeletal structure of the human figure; this is the framework on which everything else is built.

Figure 2 illustrates the layout of the main block masses of the figure. The influence of the laws of perspective is very important and must be considered when approaching this kind of subject.

Figure 3 illustrates the positions of overlapping contours which help to express the form of the figure and develop it from a hard, two-dimensional outline.

Figure 4 analyzes the main areas of light and shade which are used in the drawing to help represent solid form, and to create an interesting composition.

The head in the main drawing illustrates some of the points discussed earlier:
a) The artist was seated at a lower eye level than the model, so he had to give a feeling of looking up at the head. Perspective is again important here.
b) The proportions of the head were modified by this low eye level, so that care had to be taken to make the head appear normal rather than distorted.
c) The light, coming from the right front, models the major change of planes by creating areas of light and dark in which the minor plane alterations are shown by the use of halftones and reflected lights.
d) The hair is treated as a mass lying over the skull. Some lines are used to indicate the direction of growth of the hair.

The details of features are also conceived as block masses

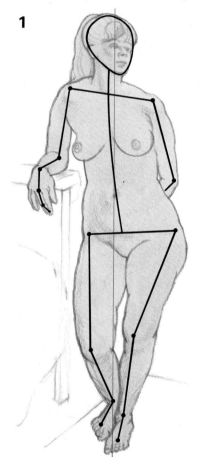

1

Above: *In this diagrammatic representation, direction is summed up with one line. Note the contrasting angles through the shoulders and pelvis, and the foreshortening in the fore-arm. The red vertical line represents the line of gravity, obtained by a plumbline to give the correct stance.*

Below: *This does not represent a style of drawing, but rather a way of thinking. Lightly sketching in these block forms may help you to see how their underlying direction governs everything else (see also pages 24 and 25). Notice here the very different direction of the volume of the head and the pelvis.*

2

3

Above: *When drawing the contours of the figure, bear in mind the areas of light and dark. This includes the background lighting as well, and the effect that this has upon the figure. The contours of the figure will be highlighted or in shadow, according to the light, and the background need not be clearly defined.*

4

which receive the same light as the underlying major plane.

Although in the analytical diagrams accompanying the drawing on page 48 the first stage is shown as being the plotting of main directions in the figure, it is not always necessary to draw in line first, with tone added later. The driving force behind your wish to make a drawing should be your emotional reaction to the subject, and this will affect your choice of technique.

Above: The amount of light and shade in drawings varies according to the pictorial idea to be expressed. Here it is used mainly in the figure to express form.

Right: In the finished drawing, as the chief aim is the study of the form of the figure, the background tones are kept to a minimum and a small amount of line and tone is used to create a sense of space around the figure. In a drawing with dramatic use of lighting to enhance the subject, there would be more use of background line and tone.

Samuel Marshall

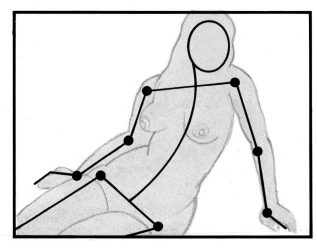

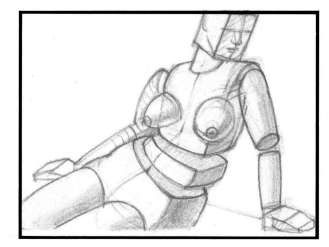

The first drawing above shows the main axial-skeletal lines superimposed onto the silhouette of the figure. These lines, as shown previously, are the basis for any figure drawing; their weight has been exaggerated here for clarity.

When beginning a drawing, keep the lines light and be ready to adjust them where necessary. If the proportions are shown correctly at this stage you will be able to concentrate later on describing form and the play of light and shade.

The second drawing shows the logical progression to form; in your studies this will be added over the top of the lightly drawn axis lines and should itself remain light in its handling. This will be refined to result in the drawing shown below.

Samuel Marshall

In this drawing the medium used was conté crayon, the main angles and directions providing the motivating force in the composition. The volumes interacted in a rhythmic way and the block forms, or combination of box and cylinder, echoed through this drawing right down to the fingers.

The adult and child study on this page was started with charcoal to establish the main masses of light and dark. This was then fixed and greater definition added with conté crayon. The design and composition of the two figures were considered extremely important, the direction of the angles of limbs, torso, and head giving an integrated and dynamic design. The large areas were blocked in before working on details of the

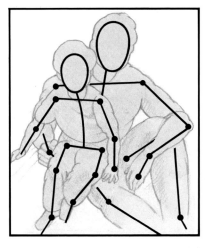

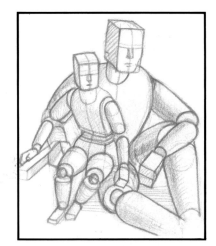

head and hands, and the direction of the light was important in showing the relief of the forms. The characteristics of both the adult and child forms and proportions were essential for this drawing.

Using charcoal, a fluid medium which is easily removed, begin the drawing with the indication of direction of form (more lightly than is shown here). Once the proportion is considered to be correct start the drawing in earnest, defining the form in a general way.

The block form shown in the second stage drawing is useful as a means by which to define the proportions and weight of the figures. If the form is drawn too wide, the figure will appear to be fat and must be trimmed down. This should be done at this stage; it will be more difficult to correct if left until later.

Alterations are now made to the basic block form of the figures to give them the appearance of specific figures as opposed to general human shapes.

Work at all times as generally as possible and do not be in too much of a hurry to draw in the detail before the form is consolidated. A generalized drawing which really appears to have solidity and weight and appears to exist in space is far more desirable than a highly detailed study which appears flat. While working do not be afraid to make alterations even if they appear to be drastic. By modifying a drawing in the light of error a more lively result is often obtained. The best drawings are the result of a continual process of refinement.

Principles of colour

Colour is one of the artist's most important means of expressing his or her personal view of the world but, as with anatomy, perspective, line, form, and tone, there are certain fundamentals which need to be understood.

The aim of studying colour from life and from theoretical principles such as the colour circle, which explains the workings of complementary colours, is that you will learn how best to exploit colour to express your own visual interpretation.

Colour in life

The nature of observed colour is a product of a variety of factors. One of the more obvious is the element of "local colour," which is the hue that belongs to the

pigmentation of the object, such as "flesh colour" or a "red blouse." Naturally, local colour pigmentation of peoples' skins or the exact red of the blouse varies considerably as do the greens in a landscape (figure 1).

When an object is solid, it can be divided into areas of light and dark, as we saw in the section concerned with tonal drawing. Figure 2 shows the local colour darkened with black and lightened with white to stress the lightness or darkness of colours. Simply adding black or white, however, can have a deadening effect on the colour, and nature is far more interesting. Even the lightest and darkest areas contain vibrant colours, due, in part, to the reflective influences of nearby colours on the shadow areas. Remember the "reflected

lights" seen in tonal drawings.

These reflected areas can change the character of the local colour. How often have you noticed the effect of colour from a jersey or blouse when reflected into the wearer's face in certain light? The colour variations and modifications can, in certain circumstances, be quite dramatic. Local colour is, therefore, always affected to some degree by the influences of colour inherent in the light source, and reflected colour from other areas (figure 3).

The colours range from warm to cool, particularly in flesh tones which reflect colour and light easily.

When using a brush, try working with as little preparatory drawing in line as possible. Draw the forms in blocks and some line. Try to cover the paper or canvas as quickly as possible with a big brush. You can only begin to relate your colours accurately when the white of the paper or canvas has disappeared.

Try also to establish a feeling of the composition and mood of the picture as soon as possible. Oil paint, acrylics, and gouache will allow repainting and redrawing into the forms with the brush. Carefully filling in a tightly drawn outline can inhibit the response to the tones and colours. The forms can be developed as the painting progresses.

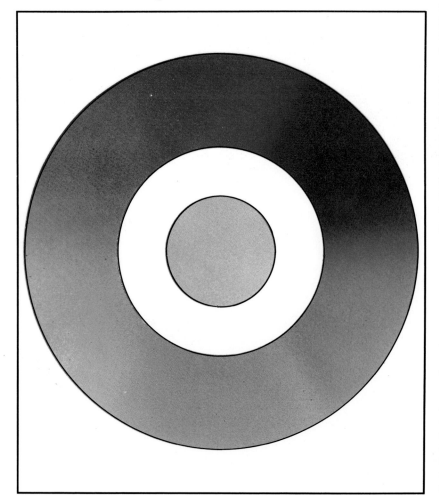

A colour circle is usually split into separate stages. Here, these blend into one another, like the colours in real life. The main parts of the circle, the primaries (pure red, yellow and blue), can be defined. The secondary colour areas – orange, green and purple – lie between. Next come the tertiaries, the more subtle gradations such as red-orange, yellow-green etc.

The complementary colours appear opposite each other on the circle. These are colours which complement and balance each other, such as green and red. Mixing complementary colours, without using black, can produce neutrals or greys, as shown here.

Approaches to colour

It is advisable for the newcomer to painting, when working from life, to remain aware of two main approaches to colour. First, if there is a strong contrast in the tones, i.e., the darkness and lightness of the colours as we would see them in a black-and-white photograph, keep the tonal quality of the colours upper-most in your mind, not simply the degree of brightness.

Rembrandt and Carravaggio used one or two smallish areas of bright colour to contrast with full, rich modelling in light and dark of quieter colours, commonly known as *neutrals*. These are colours where the emphasis lies on their tonal values; they are not colours with black added but are mixed from other colours.

Left: *This shows the sort of range of colour that Rembrandt would have used in his palette for the painting below. Here the range in tone is very wide, but the range of colour is not so great.*

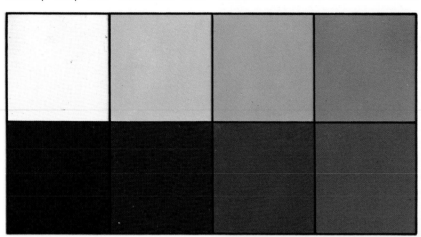

Right: *Rembrandt's* Woman Bathing *is a brilliant example of the artist's rich, deep tonality of colour, exploring the full range of the palette from light to very dark. Apart from the hint of pure red and yellow in the cloth behind the figure, the painting comprises a rich variety of more neutral tones, and indeed the whole design is conceived tonally. Rembrandt often emphasized the light areas of his paintings and here the woman's figure and chemise are built up with thick impasto brush strokes, to recreate the volume of the figure, while he has made use of thinner glazes in the darker passages of the painting.*

The second approach to painting is where the model and background make a composition which is somewhat flatter in tonal contrasts and appears similar to a mosaic. Here, a pattern of pure, or brighter, colours are laid on to emphasize, through their interaction, the "saturation" or brilliance of colour areas. Each colour used does, of course, possess its own tonal value, but these are subordinated by the overall effect.

The two methods of approach were employed by van Gogh.

He originally used a Dutch palette of similar, muted colours, but was affected by his meetings with the Impressionists. His earlier *Potato Eaters* is a rich, tonally dramatic work, while his later self portraits typify the use of purer colour in modelling form.

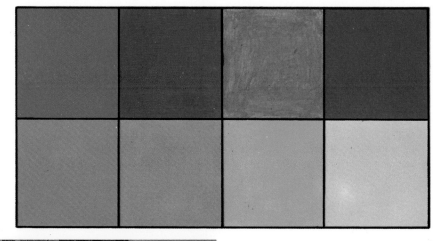

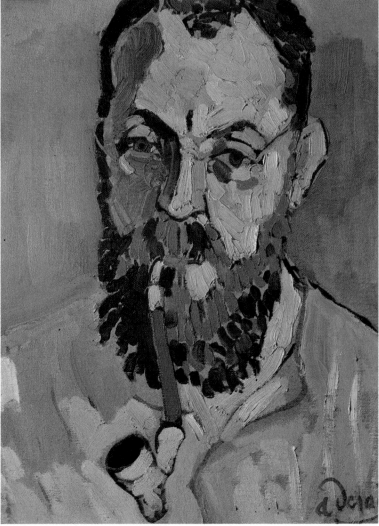

The clothed figure

The crucial factor in drawing the clothed figure is that it has a solid body beneath the clothing. Simply copying surface effects, and painstakingly representing every fold, will not necessarily produce this impression. We have to look for the areas where the body masses support the clothing and thus reveal themselves at the surface, and it is at this point that the understanding of the "blocks" of the figure's volume becomes really important.

In a standing figure, the main areas of support for the clothes are the shoulders and the waist. When the figure bends or sits, other portions become the supports. A useful clue to the nature of folds is to observe a piece of cloth hanging on a line when the folds radiate out from the points of support.

The drawing of two seated figures (opposite) shows how the major planes of the underlying forms affect the surface form of the clothing, and how actions like the man's forward-extended right arm and leg create folds which radiate out from the point of support. When properly observed and drawn they help to express the form by the way in which they twist around it.

The expression of form in the woman's left shoulder is helped by the folds caused by her left arm pressing against the upper torso. Notice the broad planes of her back beneath the clothing, and the large folds of her dress pulling from the top plane of her thigh.

Below: *The figures here clearly show how the form beneath acts as a support for the clothing. The light areas indicate the points of support, where the clothing clings more closely: the shoulders, breasts and across the hips. On the seated figure, it also clings to the thigh and upper leg. Notice also how parts of the hair mass echo the underlying form of the skull and reveal its shape, particularly on the crown of the head.*

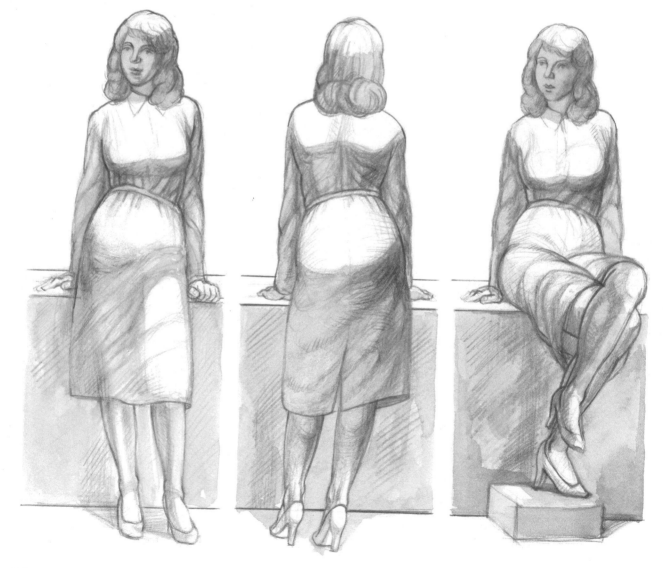

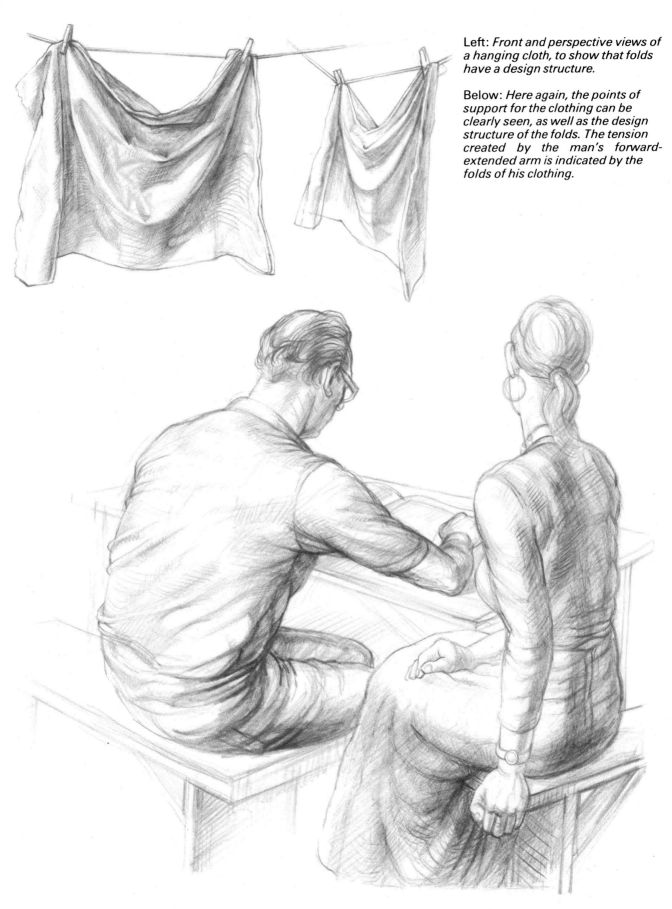

Left: *Front and perspective views of a hanging cloth, to show that folds have a design structure.*

Below: *Here again, the points of support for the clothing can be clearly seen, as well as the design structure of the folds. The tension created by the man's forward-extended arm is indicated by the folds of his clothing.*

Expressing volume

As the basic forms of trouser legs or sleeves and the body of shirts or blouses are fundamentally cylindrical, their ends or seams can help to describe the form of the figure (figure 1). Some lines going round the form, like a watchstrap around a wrist (figure 2) are comparatively tight, and so describe the "section" of the figure very clearly. This can also happen on closely worn clothing, like a shirt collar and tie (figure 6) or a roll-neck sweater (figure 4), and they are very useful for expressing the three-dimensional quality.

Other clothing which is fairly loosely worn, though not lying close to the form, can still help to express volume. Sometimes part of an edge of a sleeve or hem of a dress can lie close to the figure to provide a contour. Lines made by clothing which run down the body are just as useful in describing the figure, if only by describing the middle line (figure 3).

Pattern in clothing can assist greatly in reflecting the "terrain" of the form; stripes can act as ready-made contours. Stripes and patterns should always be drawn with an eye to the form, whether in line or tone. Notice, for instance, how the distance between stripes seems to diminish as they approach the edges of the form before disappearing around the back (figure 4).

Think of hats and caps as being projections of the skull. The brim should help to express the form of the head as it passes around the forehead and sides (figures 5 and 7).

1

2

3

4

5

Above, left and opposite: *Virtually anything that encircles a body, from a wrist watch to the neck of a sweater, can be used to define the form beneath. Keep in mind that materials vary in the way in which they react to movement. Consider the folds of clothing carefully – they can give life to a drawing or destroy its reality depending upon their positioning and they way in which they are drawn.*

6 **7**

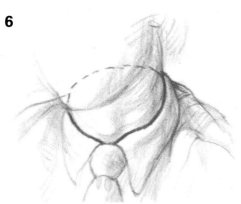

Above: *This sketch illustrates the visualization of form and volume. The concept must be kept in mind at all times while drawing or the results will look flat and unconvincing.*

Right: *In this figure study, the head and hat are more highly finished than the rest of the figure. The body retains its solidity, however, because the form was considered from the outset.*

8

Expressing movement

In vigorous action, the movement of folds and the thrusting outwards of the underlying form is much more accentuated than in a static figure (figure 8). Start by blocking in the direction lines and volumes of the body, and then draw the main movements of folds over the top. With practice in observing the direction and design of folds, imaginative figures can be constructed convincingly.

Try making observational drawings of figures in movement in your sketchbook continually, as this will teach you to grasp the essentials of movement quickly. Then build up these figures more completely from memory, trying to retain the important planes and folds.

Finally, the characteristic quality of certain kinds of clothing materials influences the extent to which the form is revealed. Stiff materials tend to wrinkle in an angular way and they resist movement somewhat. Soft, light materials, such as silk, show the underlying form more clearly.

1

2

3

4

1. The first stage is to broadly map in the proportion of the figure, painting it with a dilute cobalt blue which will eventually lose itself in the application of tone (checking a vertical line from the eye to the floor to make sure of a correct relationship with the ankle).

2. The second stage is to wash in a dilute solution of colour, approximating the local colour of the figure, clothes and background so that the white areas are largely covered with some tone. Then begin to model the form.

3. In the third stage, the modelling is developed further and the tone and colour are worked to make an increasingly exact equivalent with the subject. Pattern is treated in broad areas as well, to be drawn into and defined more exactly in the next stage. In the earlier stages, view the figure with eyes half closed in order to see the composition as broad areas of colour or tone.

4. The painting is completed by treating the tone and colour more opaquely until a satisfactory relationship is achieved. It is only in the latter stages that you should begin to include any detail.

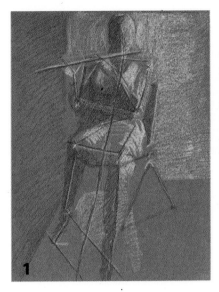

1

2

3

4

1. *First determine the main line of action of the body and the limbs, as shown. Draw rough lines to relate the joints: the tilt of the shoulders, the elbow, knee and ankle. Try to see the underlying form and draw in a vague indication of the form, showing the light on it.*

2. *In the second stage, build onto the form to develop the solidity, without concentrating on any particular area. Choose overall colours for the shadow blocks and mark them in, without indicating them too heavily as yet.*

3. *Consolidate the form further by introducing more colour where observed. The areas of darker shadow should be indicated more positively. You can now take more care over the subtleties of the figure, but do not neglect the underlying form.*

4. *The drawing is completed by the addition of more colour and now bolder lines can be used, particularly in finishing the background. Make final adjustments to the areas of light and shade. Finally, the detail can be worked in on the face, the flute and the folds of the clothes.*

Sketching

Whether or not your main interest is in drawing posed subjects, you should devote as much time as possible to working from the world at large. Firstly, working from the posed model, though essential for learning the basic language of forms, is artificial by nature, and can result in the acquisition of drawing "habits," styles, and mannerisms. We tend to select the same viewpoints or those safely within our known abilities.

Everybody needs the vigorous and invigorating unpredict-ability of everyday life to stretch their capabilities. There is little time to worry about style when drawing moving figures and, in striving to capture the key lines, masses, and tones, we have to shed many of our preconceptions and visual inhibitions.

Finding a subject

To start with, however, it is advisable to select subjects that are not so ambitious that the novice will become discouraged, and to make a number of swift studies before tackling another subject. Alternatively, keep returning to favourite themes with both quick and more highly finished drawings from as many different viewpoints as possible. Do not worry about the drawings having the same degree of accuracy as would be achieved with a posed subject, but search for other qualities, such as economy of line or expressive pattern of form.

It is not necessary to travel far to find suitable subjects for sketching; family, friends, and your immediate environment offer excellent opportunities for characterization, movement, and action. Always try to capture people in natural situations such as sewing, cooking, playing games, and so on.

Below: *This linear drawing, with soft pencil, was caught in about ten minutes, just before bedtime. Notice the girl's posture, and her air of reverie.*

Opposite above: *A tonal drawing, with the tonal area emphasized quickly and boldly with a soft pencil, as the lighting was important. Again, notice how the posture has been caught.*

Opposite below: *A sheet from a sketchbook. Babies are a good subject for sketching practice; you must be quick and bold and ready to catch their movements.*

Sam Marshall.

Learn from sketching

An important function of sketching is to explore the limits of your technical abilities, as well as to learn more of the nature of forms. False starts, failures, various "scribbles" are all natural components in a growing sketchbook, and all have a contribution of some kind to make. Decisions and execution should always be swiftly made, with emphasis placed more on the instinctively felt angles across shoulders and hips, the axial directions of limbs and torso, the sway of a garment against the tension and relaxation of underlying muscles. There is no time for slow, deliberate appraisal of proportion or outline, and the mind must work faster than the hand. Try to work unnoticed as much as possible. This will minimize self-consciousness in both your subject and yourself. You can often work inconspicuously from hidden vantage points or from behind an open newspaper in a train, bus, or café.

Avoid flicking your eyes

rapidly from subject to drawing pad, as this will attract attention as well as interrupt your own concentration. Take long, infrequent looks, committing your subject to memory before drawing. This will also help to develop your visual memory. Aim for a certain number of sketchbook drawings per week and be ambitious. One hundred would not be too many when most of them will be quick sketches.

The materials for sketching are simple. There are many makes of sketchpads on the market, in a variety of sizes. Even if you like working on a large scale, select a small pad which can be carried in pocket or handbag in addition. Experiment and use a range of materials: pencils, charcoal, inks, and chalks. Choose materials which you can easily carry in a box or cloth roll.

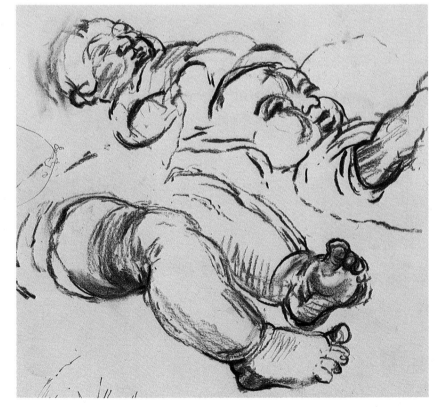

Advanced techniques

There are many instances in drawing where what we want to express demands a direct fluency and variety of line which a pencil is unable to give. The possibilities of linear variety with pen or brush and ink are wide-ranging; a stylus or technical drawing pen produces a delicate but unvarying line, felt-tipped pens can range from thick to thin, dip pens can produce a sensitive line varying from thin to broad, according to the degree of pressure.

Try making lines in all these media, including charcoal and pastel, on different papers to get the feel of them. Make a mental note of their diverse expressive qualities. A thick, jagged line, for example, is very rich and powerful and can impart emphasis and solidity to a drawing. In contrast, smooth, curving lines can suggest elegance and a subtle sensuality.

Different thicknesses of line in a drawing are very desirable, as they can impart a feeling of depth and space. For example, if the seated model's knee near the artist is drawn heavily and with emphasis in relation to the lighter linear drawing in the torso behind the leg, the line will create the feeling of the knee coming forward from the torso.

In addition, empathy plays a vital role: variety of line is something which comes naturally if we physically "feel" what the model is doing, almost as though we are "acting" the pose in sympathy. A model may be supporting her whole body weight on one leg, the other being very relaxed, for instance. If we enact this to ourselves, we should feel the line biting into the paper with great emphasis when drawing the supporting leg, as opposed to the quieter line made for the other leg. This empathy is just as important in drawing planes and volumes.

Sometimes a line is not sufficient even in a quick, direct sketch. Pen and wash has long been a medium for swift and economical statements of form: Rembrandt was one of its greatest exponents. With a few strongly felt, but carefully selected, strokes of the brush, planes, volume, and atmosphere can all be suggested to lend substance to a line drawing. It can also be used to contribute atmosphere to charcoal and conté drawings.

Wash and watercolour drawing requires some practice in laying down areas of wash and gradated tone in order to familiarize yourself with the inherent quality and directness of the medium, but the results can be well worth the effort.

Below: *This drawing with a soft pencil illustrates the use of a variety of smooth curving lines to help express the languorous pose.*

Left: *This detail shows the use of mixed media, including charcoal, pastel and some gouache. It is a complete, imaginative figure composition, inspired mainly from memory. The thickness of the line on the foreground figures is made much heavier and more angular by the use of a brush and chalk, to help express the volume. This is in contrast with the more dreamlike figures in the background. The original is a large scale drawing (52'' x 48''), which started with charcoal and gradually built up to paint to acquire definition.*

Below: *This is a brush drawing using a watercolour wash technique. No preliminary drawing was made and the emphasis is on the calligraphic handling of the brush, to just suggest the body and the hair. The background is hardly defined at all and the design and atmosphere of the drawing culminates in the head, where the face is slightly in shadow.*

Appreciation

Great figure drawings are extremely diverse in conception and execution, as can be seen from the works of Michelangelo, Matisse, Rembrandt, Picasso, Dürer, Schiele, Rodin, Hokusai, and Holbein. They are all very different and yet all have the power to move us deeply. The quality which they all have in common is the revelation of certain spiritual or emotional truths expressed with conviction.

As the artists matured, many of their drawings became increasingly subjective: forms and proportions could be grossly exaggerated in order to emphasize certain moods or impressions. Look at later works by Picasso and Matisse. Many seem to have been set down in a few minutes, and many great drawings do not exemplify standards of "normal" or "accepted" beauty. Many nudes appear as a gross contradiction of contemporary standards of health or beauty: Egon Schiele's models were often emaciated

(or at least the expressive aspects of the drawings make them appear to be so), while Ruben's female ideal is far from the accepted norm of today.

The power of the drawings, however, lies in the dynamic and expressive quality resulting from a successful marriage between spiritual insight and the visual relationships between the qualities of line, tone, volume, and space.

A drawing is often only concerned with the visual interaction of abstract qualities, and indeed, all great figure drawings possess this integration of visual fact and energy as the "plastic" vehicle for emotional expression. As a result, it is often impossible to separate content from form whether the technique is figurative or abstract. The best drawings are never purely descriptive, and the forms have an abstract life of their own. In many sculptor's drawings, including those of

Above: *Degas is one of the great figure "draughtsmen" of all time. In* Woman Drying Herself *the movement, the complete pictorial design, the pattern of light and dark and the volume in the figure itself are all beautifully observed.*

Left: *Sargent brought tremendous drawing powers to his painting. In* Study of Mme. Gautreau *he emphasizes the linear drawing with his brush, treating the figure at first as a silhouette against the background.*

Henry Moore, the drawings are primarily about the volumes of the figure, and the thrust and recession of forces within.

No time spent studying the aspects of the human figure outlined in this book through your own analytical drawings will be wasted; it will provide you with the means to make your own authoritative and highly individual statements about the qualities you see in the world and the subjects you tackle.